The Vapor

Bryna Bar Oni

THE VAPOR

Visual Impact, Inc.
500 S. Clinton St.
Chicago, IL 60607

Library of Congress Catalog Card Number: 76–619
ISBN: 0–913426–03–2 (clothbound)

This book is dedicated to the blessed
  memory of my dear father, Itzchok Ben
  Joseph Ben Faiga
my mother, Malka Leah Bath Jacob Bath
  Chaja
my sister, Yentl
my sister, Henia, to whom my sister Dalya
  and I owe our lives
my younger brother, Chaim
my brother-in-law, Lejba
my niece, Rochele
my nephew, Matys

They were all killed by the Nazis; some in
  the Byten ghetto and some in the
  woods.

My everlasting love to my sister Dalya.

Contents

Family portrait. The author (standing on chair) and her sister, Dalya (holding bouquet), were survivors of the holocaust. Her parents and her older sisters, Yentl (l.) and Henia (r.), lost their lives. Also murdered was her brother, Chaim, not yet born in 1929 when this photograph was taken.

Foreword

Before Israel, Eastern European Jews maintained a sense of community and identity by living together in small towns, or shtetls. The way of life I experienced in my hometown, Byten, was typical of that in other shtetls. Only government officials—the mayor, the post office director, the police, the teachers, along with their assistants—were Gentile. Although peasants from the surrounding countryside would flock into town on Sundays to their churches and on market days to sell their goods, most activity in town reflected Jewish law and custom. And we shtetl Jews frowned on the "cosmopolitan Jews" who foresook their people and religion to become assimilated in urban cultures. Because the shtetl way of life no longer exists anywhere in the world, I have devoted one chapter of *The Vapor* to my life before World War II.

Americans often ask, "Why was it that six million Jews allowed themselves to be led, unprotesting, to their deaths?" To understand the answer, it is necessary to understand the full horror of the holocuast. There were some who resisted but their story, until now, has remained largely untold. That is why I have chosen to set forth, in some detail, the experiences of Polish Jews who fought as partisans.

I consider it significant, though incredible, that Hitler

and his henchmen could remain detached from the suffering they caused. Perhaps it is this inability to identify with suffering of others that enables human beings to inflict pain on others—particularly on those different from themselves —and keeps the world constantly at war.

I write of my personal nightmare in the hope that its revelation in the light of a day thirty years later may help prevent its happening again.

It is no easy task I am asking of you, the reader: to experience, as I have experienced; to weep, as I have wept; to deplore, as I have deplored, our inhumanity to each other.

But tears can be purifying.

B.B.C.

Part One: My home

1

I am Bryna, the seventh child of a Jewish family of eight. I was born in Poland in 1925. My mother's father was a ritual slaughterer, an extremely pious man. He had three sons, whom he educated to be rabbis, and five daughters who were bright and spirited despite their lack of formal schooling. They were also quite beautiful.

But grandfather was poor, so none of his daughters married men of prestige. Since it was the custom in Europe for parents to give each daughter a dowry upon her marriage and since the size of the dowry depended on the wealth of the parents, wealthy girls tended to marry wealthy men. Mother's young man was a mill builder by trade, as his father and forefathers had been. They were married in 1905, when she was 19. Father's work kept him away most of the time and we saw him mainly on holidays. Mother was kept busy operating a drygoods store and raising children.

Tall and striking, witty and wise, mother was also inclined to be vehement. Those who knew her said that if women could be elected to the Senate she most certainly would be. My father, a man of slight stature, had delicate features—blue eyes deeply set below a wide forehead, a straight nose—adorned by a small black mustache and tiny pointed beard. His calm, phlegmatic disposition was quite

the opposite of my mother's. He was skeptical of en-
thusiasm, easily satisfied, gullible, honest and quiet.
Because of the differences in their temperaments, my
parents were far from being an ideal couple. The truth is,
they were not too happy with each other.

My father's artisan way of life was no match for my
mother's sharp ability in practical affairs, and they frequently disagreed about business problems. Mother was
almost always right in her judgment, and she did not
hesitate to point this out to my father. Father was a bright
man, but in a different way. He was a skillful mechanic, a
builder of grain mills, and he designed and built machinery
for the manufacture of cereals and flour. He could read a
blueprint and was an excellent carpenter. Often engineers
would consult my father when they encountered difficulties. Once an important engineer from Warsaw built
a big grain mill which, when finished, would not function.
He consulted other engineers, but none could find fault
with the structure. Finally it was suggested that he speak
with my father. Father took one look at the mill and sur-
mised that the chimney was too short; it simply did not
provide enough draft. At my father's suggestion the
chimney was lengthened and the problem was solved.

Finally, although he was then in middle age, father
decided he wanted to own a mill himself. He found one for
sale in Byten, a small town 50 kilometers north of
Baranowicze. His plan was to move our family as soon as
possible. Mother was dead set against this. One day I came
home from kindergarten and found her in a fit of anger.
Her face flushed and her voice high-pitched, she was
screaming at father; "With four daughters and two of them
ready for marriage, you want to move to Byten, that God-
forsaken hole in the middle of nowhere? What future will
our daughters have to look forward to?

"Even those who live there tell us to think twice before

we buy the mill. With the wells dried up, where do you think we're going to get water to operate the steam engine? You are a stubborn fool, Itzchok!"

To father, the rundown mill presented a challenge as well as an opportunity for independence. He was sure that he could correct its ills, and he kept insisting that mother share his confidence in his abilities. The quarrel continued for a few weeks before father emerged the winner. I, though hardly five years old, had the feeling that mother was the one who was right.

Our departure from Baranowicze and the home we all loved remains vivid in my mind. We moved slowly through the countryside, six of us and our belongings packed into a horse-drawn wagon. After a day and night of traveling, we finally arrived at Byten, nestled in the valley of the Szczara River. The sound of wheels on the cobblestone street echoed in the early-morning stillness as we passed the shops in the center of town. At the end of the street, on the side of a hill, stood my father's grain mill—a wooden two-story building with a high chimney and a huge yard filled with rows of chopped wood. Across from the mill was a fenced lot that served as a kettle market.

A few hundred yards from the mill was our new home, its construction typical of many in small Polish towns. The entrance to the one-story house was through a big front porch. A white tiled oven, high to the ceiling, divided the house into four rooms and heated each one. There was another hearth oven in the kitchen for baking bread or putting up a *cholent* (dinner) for the Sabbath, and in front of it was a place for frying food or boiling water for tea. Underneath the hearth was a chicken coop, placed there so chickens wouldn't freeze in wintertime. The house was painted with white calcimine inside and out. It had many windows and wooden floors painted red, which we rubbed with a red pomade every month to achieve a glossy luster.

The pantry room had only a dirt floor. A wing of the roof in the pantry could be moved by a special contraption, and it was open to the sky during the *Succoth* holidays.

The side door of the porch led to a big yard, where there was a cellar. Only the shingled roof of the cellar was above ground. There we kept potatoes, cabbage and radishes through the winter, and dairy products, meats and vegetables in the summer. Next to the cellar were the wooden toilet and an old barn for storing wood and sheltering livestock. Outside the bedroom windows grew plum and pear trees and potatoes. Behind the potato patch was a Jewish blacksmith's forge, where farmers would bring horses to be shod; plows, sickles, rakes and knives to be sharpened, and wagon wheels, hinges, knobs and latches to be forged. Every morning we were awakened by the blacksmith's hammering.

Byten had five forges in all. Sometimes on a quiet day I could hear the town's rhythm being hammered out on the anvils by the calloused hands of the Jewish blacksmiths. That rhythm became for a symbol of sweat and honest work.

Every month our town was livened by the hustle and bustle of the market day. The town became festive, with peasants from surrounding villages bringing in products to sell and buying things they could not grow or make themselves. Their wagons were loaded with sacks of potatoes, grain, geese and fruit. Under big homespun shawls, the peasant women carried chickens, dishes of butter and baskets of eggs.

At the wagons the Jewish women of the town picked up the chickens one by one, blowing at their feathers to see if the skin was yellow—if they had enough fat. Blue chickens were the old ones and they didn't make very good soup. As the chickens clucked and the ducks quacked, the bargaining went on—often between two women:

"How much do want for the chicken?"

"Three zlotys!"

"What? You want to skin me? Here is one zloty." She waves it before the peasant's eyes. The eyes do not waver. "Well, I'll give you another half zloty. Is it a bargain?"

"You're wasting my time."

"You are a stubborn mule. I'll tell you what: let's split the difference."

A woman would pick up perhaps a dozen chickens until she was satisfied with her choice.

The market square, so crowded you had to elbow your way through, had special corners for bisque pottery, saddler's goods, wheels, sickles and various household supplies. The noisiest corner was where ready-made clothes, sheepskin jackets and pieces of rubber tires with leather laces (used for shoes by peasants) were sold. The merchants' shrill voices boasted about the merchandise; the bargaining was deafening.

I remember a typical incident. A peasant tried on a jacket and thought it too large for him. There was no mirror, so the merchant, anxious to make a sale, pulled the jacket up in the back. Excitedly, he told the peasant: "It fits perfectly and you certainly cut a nice figure in it."

"The sleeves are too long," retorted the peasant.

Lifting the jacket at the shoulders, the merchant shouted: "Straighten up. Now you see, the sleeves are the right size! You are getting a bargain in this jacket. I can never replace it for this money, but business is slow, and at home I have a family to feed. And what about my horse? He wants to eat, too. Grab the jacket before I change my mind." The peasant, gullible and confused, argued about the price but finally bought the jacket. The merchant had reason to be desperate. To get to the market he traveled one day and one night over sandy dirt roads. He had to bear the cost of maintaining a horse and buggy, and at home there was a large family to sustain. His lot was not an easy one.

Our town itself had many little stores, and the store-keepers, too, found it hard to eke out a living. On market days they would stand in the doorways of their stores, pulling at the farmers, enticing them to buy a pinch of salt, sugar or spices, and babushkas for their womenfolk to wear to church on Sundays. Observing the fierce competition of the storekeepers, I was glad, in a way, that we had a mill. There were only two mills in our town. Still, the other mill was so well established and so efficiently run, we could never truly compete with it.

Byten had three liquor stores and they enjoyed tremendous business on market days. Before the peasant departed for home, he stopped to indulge himself in the luxury of 100 percent spirit vodka, a loaf of white bread and a large, salty herring. He felt happy then. After eating and drinking lustily, he returned home in a drunken stupor, most probably to beat his wife. On Sundays, too, while the womenfolk went to church, the peasant men got drunk. I usually was in mortal fear when the drunken peasants, singing their sad songs, passed by our home on their way back to their villages, occasionally breaking windows and engaging in other vandalism. What I liked were the ballads the peasants sang on Sunday evenings. I could hear their songs coming from surrounding villages, some as far as five kilometers away.

As soon as we arrived in Byten, father began getting the mill ready. He built machinery for grinding barley, oats, buckwheat—all kinds of grain. He shaped the huge cement stones and, later, with a sharp chisel, he incised the semi-circular grooves that ground the rye to flour. While father took care of the technical operations of the enterprise, mother managed both the business and the family. She would get up at four to do the cooking for the whole day. After we had our breakfast and left for school, she had to carry water from the well in our back yard and firewood from the barn. In winter when the wood was cold and hard, this chore was especially difficult.

The mill did not bring the happiness father expected. Mother had been right about the problems. With the mill on sandy, hilly terrain, it was difficult to get enough water for the steam engine. Three wells were dug and expensive pumps installed, but they could not reach the water level. Sometimes my parents had to get up during the night to draw water by hand to fill the two big reservoirs for the next day's operation. Before market days, even though I was only 10 years old, I would get up at night to draw bucket after bucket of water. We also hired peasants to bring water in barrels from the nearby river. It hurt me to see how hard my parents had to work and I lent my hand whenever I could.

The Polish government only added to our family's trouble. The increasing anti-Semitism showed itself in various ways, especially through the levying of unusually heavy taxes on the Jews. Most families could meet their tax obligations only through the help of relatives in the United States. Almost every family had at least one relative from whom it constantly received favors.

Mother cried for months after her first-born son, Nathan, left Poland at the age of 15. (Her second son, Pinchus, had died of dysentery during World War I.) But the calamity became a blessing, because Nathan was a big help to us whenever our fortunes at home were at a low ebb.

One time, thieves broke into our mill and got away with many sacks of flour that belonged to shopkeepers. My father was brought before the *Din Torah* (court of arbitration) at the rabbi's house, where two citizens pronounced judgment. The decision of the *Din Torah* was that my father was responsible for the safekeeping of the grain brought to his mill for grinding. Our plight was serious because our own grain had been stolen, too. Nathan saved us by sending money to pay off the shopkeepers.

Another time, thieves stole the main transmission belt that connected the steam engine to the machines in the mill. The belt, which was made from camel skin, was expensive, and a replacement could be bought only in Warsaw or Wilno. The mill was idle for a couple of months, until Nathan could send the necessary funds. In the meantime, my parents had to pay wages to the machinist and the miller boy as well as care for the five of us at home.

We were a closely knit family, very devoted to each other. In addition, our home was always open to visitors, and we often had guests at our table. Whoever passed through town was likely to stay at our house—a Zionist speaker, a *meshulach* collecting money for religious schools, or a *chazon* (cantor) coming to sing at the religious services. Sometimes on Saturdays, my father would bring a wandering hobo home to dinner, and my mother, not knowing, would also ask a guest.

On Friday, at the time of the blessing of the Sabbath candles, our mill sounded a siren and all of the shops closed their businesses until the next Monday morning. Nobody trespassed on the holiness of the Sabbath, the day of rest and prayer, and on Sunday the businesses again had to be closed, according to the law of the land. (The synagogues in Poland were orthodox; the women sat apart from the men.)

My sister, Henia, was very good in the business. She took care of the books and, on Fridays, helped out in the mill while mother baked the *chalah* (white egg bread), *zemel* (sweet rolls) and *strudel* and made the *zimmes* (meat with carrots and plums) which was left overnight in an oven and eaten on Saturday after the synagogue services. Since the Jews could not light the oven on Saturday, the food was kept warm this way for the next day's dinner.

Besides being an excellent business woman, mother was a talented cook. Her gefilte fish on Friday night was most delectable. As head of the family, father would get the head portion of the fish. On Fridays, the table was set with a crisp tablecloth and the good china. Two large braided *chalahs* for *Kiddush* (a prayer thanking God for the Sabbath) adorned the table on one side, with the Sabbath candles on the other. Mother, when she blessed the candles, said her own personal prayer, asking the Almighty's blessing on her family and relief from her troubles.

Most of the time a peasant woman came to scrub and polish the wooden floors. The linens were changed on Friday and all of us had to wash our hair and take a bath. We went to the mill for baths because there we had a huge tin bathtub that we could fill with hot water from the steam engine.

I was proud of my sisters, for they were so beautiful. Yentl, the oldest, was tall, slim, with long, light brown wavy hair, powder blue eyes, a straight nose with a cleft in it, and another cleft in her chin. She sang beautifully, with much feeling, and her repertory included religious songs, Polish tangos and popular Jewish numbers. Her voice was so powerful that window panes shook. Neighbors stood under our windows to listen.

Henia had a complexion like a china doll and her eyes reflected her spirit and wisdom. She had a peculiar, yet pleasant, laugh, full of vitality.

Both of my older sisters were students of Hebrew, having graduated from the Hebrew school in Baranowicz. Both had trouble adjusting to the provincial life in Byten. Byten's residents had limited education. There was no high school in town—just the seven-grade public school and the Hebrew school, *Talmud Torah*, housed in the Chassidic *shtible* or synagogue.

Gradually, however, Henia and Yentl began participating in local social life. In the evenings Henia liked to play chess. Several evenings a week, both sisters and my Hebrew teacher, Jankle Uzelewsky, who had an eye for Henia, would study the *Torah* and its commentaries. They subscribed to various Hebrew publications and the daily Jewish newspaper, the *Moment*. My sisters were active in the *Bikur Cholim*, the organization that provided help to the sick and volunteers to care for them. Byten did not have a hospital or a dentist and did not always have a medical doctor. In emergencies, *Bikur Cholim* provided money so that the poor of the town could get medical help in big cities nearby. At burials, the family had to give *tzdokah* (charity) to keep up the Jewish cemetery. A certain percentage of the money was funneled to *Bikur Cholim* and to *Hachnosat Calah* (a group that would help poor brides meet their wedding expenses.) My sisters also gave to the monthly collections for *Keren Kayemet*, *Keren Hayesod* (the Jewish National Fund) for the reclamation of the land of Israel. My parents contributed to the *Moas Chitim* relief for the poor and to the *Gamilat Chassidim*, a loan association where a needy person could borrow up to 50 zlotys.

As a whole, life in our small town held more rags than riches. This was true of eastern Poland generally and for the farmers as well as the small-town people. Many families were dependent on the community for the bare necessities of life. Yet being poor did not make people feel underprivileged. Neither did it give them an inferiority complex.

Even though their parents were often recipients of charity, my girl friend, Chana Lubersky, and her twin brother were very popular with the young crowd. Most of the time they lived on buttermilk and potatoes. Chana was a pretty girl with refined manners, the best singer in the class, and highly intelligent. Her brother was full of spunk. Their father was a *bal hagolah*, a wagoner, whose delicate health prevented him from making a decent living in his profession. I remember Mrs. Lubersky coming to my mother to borrow a pair of shoes to wear when she had to go out of town for the burial of her mother.

Another friend, Basha Noznicka, was the daughter of a baker. The prettiest girl in town, she was chased by all the young men. She was a good actress in the dramatic society, able to laugh or cry at will. Yet, at age nine, she had to help her family—baking bread and rolls after school, weeding the vegetable garden in the summer. Basha was an object of envy because she had received a visa from her grandmother in Argentina and was making plans to live there. (Unfortunately her dreams were shattered. World War II broke out and Basha was incarcerated in the barbed-wire ghetto. Later, she was raped and killed.)

Like other small Jewish towns in Poland, Byten attracted speakers from various Zionist organizations. Their speeches and debates took place at the fire department barracks. Very often the debates were interrupted by members of opposing Zionist factions. Quarrels broke out and chairs would fly.

The fire department barracks were also used as a theater. Here, the local dramatic society and traveling groups of artists presented performances relating to Jewish life. *The Dibuk* (exorcist), *Tevye, the Milchiger* (a story similar to *Fiddler on the Roof*), *The Wandering Jew* and other tragic or sentimental works made the women and children weep profusely. They would come out of the theater with red swollen eyes, the songs and episodes of the plays haunting them for a long, long time. The more they cried, the better they liked the play.

Often the plot revolved around a husband leaving for America. He carried with him the idea of making easy money and sending for his family as soon as he was settled and became a citizen. Instead, in the process of Americanization, he forgot his family, and his wife and children remained lonesome and in poverty.

Sometimes the story took another twist: the son, a cantor in the synagogue, leaves for America and becomes a renowned opera singer. Success goes to his head and he disassociates himself from his family. Following a pogrom by the Hungarian Cossacks, his widowed mother is brought to America by the *Hias* (an American Jewish charity group organized to help immigrants.) Disembarking in America, she sees a poster with her son's picture on it, advertising his concert. She goes to the performance. It is, indeed, her son! She is proud to see her Yankele (or Shmuelke) move the audience so much that they give him a tumultuous ovation. When he walks past her down the aisle, she tries to stop him by holding on to the tails of his coat. He looks with contempt at the old woman in rags. He does not recognize his mother. The heartache is too much for her to bear, and she dies right there of a heart attack.

Because entertainment was scarce in our town, reading was a favorite pastime. Byten was proud of its libraries. The Peretz library, founded by efforts of the trade unions in 1902, and the Brenner Library, founded in the 1930s and supported by Jewish Relief societies in New York, were stacked with more than 1,500 books. As youngsters on Saturday afternoons in summer, we used to gather in the shade of the old linden trees in the little park and read books about other countries and cultures. Filled with great expectations, we dreamed of travel and romanticized our future.

Another favorite place to rendezvous was near the Polish and White Russian cemeteries, about a kilometer out of town. There was a beautiful walkway between the trees and the grain fields. The brush and shrubbery screened from public view the young people in love.

The most exciting regular event in Byten was the Saturday afternoon promenade on Zarechte street. The street, which started at the bell tower, was lined on both sides with weeping willows and led to the bridge over a streamlet. Here, all paraded in their very best, displaying fine clothes of the season. My sisters, Yentl and Henia, used to go to Baranowicze to order wardrobes according to the latest Paris fashions. Yentl was the first one to wear a dress up to her ankles when long dresses came in vogue. That Saturday afternoon she was the talk of the town. People pointed at her and said, "There goes the miller's daughter."

Although I was hurt and ashamed, I could detect envy in their voices.

On weekdays along the same street, the washerwomen carried big braided, straw baskets filled with washed and boiled clothes to be rinsed in the clear water of the streamlet. Here also they brought their homespun linens to be bleached. Before Passover, the Jews would bring their pots and pans and silverware to be rinsed after they were made kosher by being cleansed with hot stones and boiling water.

On vacations we would cut through the fields and go swimming in the Szczara River. The women and children swam in a place separate from the men, who usually went under the bridge where the water was deep. Not all of the women owned bathing suits. At times, daring young men came close to where the women bathed. The girls would run to nearby bushes to cover up, but sometimes they let themselves be "deceived" just to enliven the beach.

The river that provided us with so much pleasure also demanded its toll. Each year somebody drowned. When our neighbor's daughter was found drowned in the river, I was too young to understand the rumor that circulated in town. The only daughter of very old parents, she had always seemed a lonely girl. The townspeople suspected that a certain young man had taken advantage of her and that she had become pregnant. Not having friends to turn to, she felt that the only alternative to giving birth to a momzer (illegitimate child) was to drown herself.

The happiest occasions in Byten were the weddings. In 1936 Yentl was married. A matchmaker arranged the marriage with a very handsome young man from another small town. Lejba was dark and six feet tall, had fiery eyes and beautiful teeth, and looked like a gypsy.

Before the wedding, mother took Yentl to the mikvah and I accompanied them. The mikvah was a huge tiled chamber filled with water where a ritualistic, purifying bath was taken. After all three of us took steam baths, mother instructed Yentl to go to the room where the *mikvah* was and submerge in the water, saying a certain prayer. When we left the bathhouse, I saw her receive a *zetl* (a written statement) affirming that she had fulfilled the *mitzvah* (commandment) of the *mikvah*, for only then would the rabbi perform the wedding ceremony.

On Friday, before sundown, she was married under the open skies in the mill yard. The wedding canopy was beautifully decorated. The yard was full of people, and the peasants from the neighboring countryside gathered beyond the mill's fence. Saturday, after synagogue services, my parents served a *kiddush* honey cake, wine herring, *zimmes* and gefilte fish, with a special table set for beggars. The Rawitzky brothers played the fiddle and called out the wedding gifts. Fifty percent of our mill was given by our parents as a dowry to Yentl. *Horahs* were danced until late in the evening.

In 1937, when I was 12 years old, I graduated from the seventh grade of the public school. I was the best student in the class, but it was not easy or pleasurable for me. I was constantly competing with two other students whom I considered superior. A boy named Bohme was a genius, and my girl friend, Golda Slonimska, had the ability to retain everything she read. My advantage was that I was quick to grasp ideas and could explain them clearly. The procedure in Polish schools called for oral and written examinations on each subject every half year. I was exempt from the oral examinations, but I had to sit in on them. When no one else in the class could answer a question, the teacher called on me. Luckily, I knew the answers because I could understand the principles involved, even though the information pertaining to the questions could not be found in the textbooks. Although this made me outstanding in school, I lacked confidence in myself and did not believe I could live up to the image the teachers had of me. I was always under great nervous strain when the examinations came.

Although our town did not have a secondary school, my parents wanted me to continue my education. The only way was to send me to Baranowicze. This involved great expense, so I stayed home for a year to earn a little money. I tutored a dozen children, charging four to five zlotys a month per child.

During the day I helped in the mill and even learned to operate the machinery that ground barley and buckwheat. I was the only girl in the family who did this kind of work. In Poland it was a disgrace for young ladies to do their own housework or even carry their shopping packages. A girl would blush with shame if a neighbor walked in and caught her in the process of washing floors or dishes. Young ladies were supposed to spend their days reading books or doing fancy embroidery.

I intensely disliked this mode of life and thought it nonsense. I didn't care for fancy clothes and can't remember owning a new dress. I didn't mind wearing clothes handed down by my older sisters. During the wintertime I was the only young girl who dressed like the farmers around us—in a sheepskin jacket and heavy felt boots, which were worn in Siberia. I used to stay in the mill all day in weather that sometimes dropped to 40 degrees below zero.

On Thursday evenings I would go shopping for Sabbath needs and I would often carry home heavy packages. On Fridays I helped wash the wooden floors in our house.

When I graduated from public school in 1937, sensational purge trials were going on in Russia. Actually, the purge had started in 1933 with the expulsion of many oldline Communists. In 1937-38 there were few old Bolsheviks left in the Central Committee. I remember headlines in the Polish newspapers about happenings in Russia, but I didn't really understand what was going on. That same year, Japan launched a full-scale invasion of China.

Until this time, life in our town had certainly not been idyllic, but it was peaceful. There was little violence; most of us were absorbed in the day-to-day business of living. In a short while, however, we would be sucked into the whirlwind of war.

Part Two: The Russian occupation

2

In 1938, tension in Europe was rapidly mounting. In March, Germany annexed Austria. In September, Hitler invited the British Prime Minister, Neville Chamberlain, and Edouard Daladier, the French premier, to a four-power conference in Munich, attended also by his henchman, Benito Mussolini of Italy. It was in Munich that Chamberlain and Daladier accepted Hitler's plan to annex part of Bohemia, a province of Czechoslovakia in which the majority of people were Germans. By this annexation, Czechoslovakia lost its mountainous approaches and fortifications and became militarily defenseless. At the conference in Munich, Hitler gave solemn guarantees to respect the integrity of what remained of Czechoslovakia. Chamberlain and Daladier were received with cheers at home when they reported that they had secured "peace in our time."

One consequence of Hitler's advances in Europe was the rise of anti-Semitism in Poland. The great dislike for Jews now became more open. Propaganda warned people not to shop in Jewish stores. On promenade streets, a Polish anti-Semitic group known as the *Andeki* cut with razor blades the fur coats of the Jewish women. Zabotynski, a Jewish leader, urged the Polish Jews to leave Poland, legally or illegally, and go to Israel: "Europe is a burning ship, and

19

there is no alternative but to leave the ship in order to survive." His opponents from other Zionist organizations attacked him bitterly, accusing him of exacerbating the already inflamed anti-Semitism in Poland.

In 1938, I left home to attend a commercial high school in Baranowicze but, when the situation worsened in 1939, I returned to Byten. The Jews in Byten lived in constant fear. Anxiously they read their newspapers and kept their ears to the radio for the latest news.

The final disillusionment regarding appeasement policies came on March 14-15, 1939. Hitler marched into Bohemia Moravia, the Czech part of Czechoslovakia, made it a German protectorate and declared Slovakia "independent." One week later, Czechoslovakia disappeared from the map. Germany seized the port city of Memel from Lithuania, the Italians conquered Albania and, in August, the Danzig-Polish crisis broke out, leading directly to war. Desperately, the British and French tried to form an anti-German alliance with Russia, but Poland and the Baltic states were unwilling to allow Soviet armies within their borders. England, France and Poland renewed their agreement which, by August, had hardened into a mutual assistance pact.

Hitler was so incensed by what he called Britain's "policy of encirclement" that Germany denounced the 10-year German-Polish Nonaggression Pact of 1934.

In the summer of 1939, the Russians waved aside Anglo-French pleas for mutual assistance. Instead, on August 23, she signed a treaty of nonaggression and friendship with Hitlerite Germany. It was secretly agreed that, in any further territorial rearrangement, Russia and Germany would divide Poland and the Baltic states between them. It was this agreement that caused Great Britain and France to declare war on Germany on September 3, 1939.

Two weeks after the Germany invasion of Poland, the Russians, acting under the secret clauses of the German-

*Soviet pact, moved into the eastern half of Poland, up to
the River Bog. They occupied an area roughly equivalent to
the territory they lost to Poland in the Russo-Polish war of
1920.*

Germany invaded Poland on September 1, 1939. The
very first day of the war, the Warsaw radio station stopped
functioning. Railway transportation and civilian communications were forbidden. All newspaper publication
stopped. Rumors were the principal sources of information.
On the third day of the war, the Moscow radio station com-
mented that only by a miracle could Poland survive.

Within a few days, Jewish refugees from central Poland
swarmed into Byten and other eastern cities of Poland.
They brought the news that there was no longer a Polish
government and that the Germans were already very near.
We saw remnants of Polish army divisions hiding in the
fields and woods, seeking any kind of protection from low-
flying German airplanes, which were making strikes on
the civilian population as well as military installations.

Having lost all contact with the central government, our
police and local civil officials became confused. For a time,
they were more friendly with the Jews. We now had
mutual enemies in the Germans. The peasants who came
from neighboring villages to buy goods from the stores were
totally calm. The population along the eastern border of
Poland was 90% White Russian. These people had never
wanted to be Polish citizens. Indeed they looked forward to
the German occupation with the hope that eventually they
would be able to form their own independent White Russian government.

Lonely and forlorn, surrounded by enemies, the Jews of
our town desperately looked for a miracle, but none oc-
curred. On Saturday, September 16, a rumor circulated
that the Germans were only 40 kilometers from Byten. Trying to find some consolation in community, the Jews
quickly filled the streets. At night we packed our belong-

ings. The shopkeepers tried to smuggle out merchandise from their stores, hiding it in pits they dug in their barns and cellars and camouflaging the hiding places with straw and cattle manure. Many Jews in Byten packed sacks with food in case they might have to flee. The young people, their bicycles loaded with sacks and packages, stood ready day and night to leave their homes.

Then came surprising news. The mayor of our town suddenly announced that the Russians were coming to our aid and that they had already occupied Baranowicze. They could be expected in Byten any minute. We were astounded by the tone of his report because the mayor was known to be unfriendly toward Jews. We felt that his attempt to calm us was merely a trick. Once again we heard rumors that the German *blitzkrieg* or "lightning warfare" had ended the resistance of the organized Polish army. Simultaneously, Moshe Witkow of our town received confirming word from a local White Russian, a Communist of the underground, that the Russians were indeed approaching.

The next day, three members of the local Communist underground approached Dodl Abramowicz, a drygoods storekeeper. They wanted red cloth from his store to make flags. They were forming committees to greet the Russian army, which was resting on the other side of the Szczara River. Three young local Communists and a small group of followers started to demonstrate in the streets. Gathering momentum as they reached the fire department barracks, they improvised a platform and began elaborating on the historic moment we were about to witness. They said that they were now free citizens, no longer under the yoke of Polish feudalists: "We will bury the Polish Fascism which brutally subjugated our brothers."

A member of the local Communist Party assumed control of the town government and ordered all stores closed so that there would be no more looting. We were told not to congregate in the streets. Guns were taken from the Polish police and given to the local Communists, who were to guide and watch over the town and the area around it.

Sunday afternoon, September 17, our town was startled by bursts of machinegun fire. The shooting seemed to come from the highway that led to Slonim. Later we learned that a high-ranking Polish officer had left a Polish troop-train which was proceeding toward Baranowicze. Trying to escape the German bombardment, he and his chauffeur passed Byten on their way to Slonim, only to encounter a barricade set up by local Communists. The officer was wounded critically, but the chauffeur managed to make his way to the town of Zyrowice, near Slonim. When he told Polish police about the shooting, he described it as an uprising in Byten. The Polish civil government was still functioning in Slonim, and within a few hours they sent a punitive expedition to our town. The Communists, meanwhile, had fled to the woods and we were hiding in our homes, afraid to step out into the lawless streets. Three chaotic days later, at ten in the evening, we finally saw the lights of the first Russian tank. The entire population went out to meet the Russians. On top of the first tank stood an officer who told us that the Polish Fascist government was demolished.

"Comrade Stalin sent us here to deliver you," he said. "Your welcome for us is your show of trust in us, but we also know that there are many among you who are our enemies. Your task is to find out who they are and bring them to us." I heard my father say to a close friend that he thought the Russians would be no better than the Germans and that no matter which side we were on, we would still be the losers. His friend looked at him in disgust and told him he had sinned by his prophecy.

Looking at the caravan of trucks and tanks of the mighty Russian army, I suddenly felt compassion for the Polish government, which I had intensely disliked because of its attitude toward the Jews who "fouled the air" and were "parasites on their country." I pitied the nation that just a few weeks before had been so proud of its glory. At the moment I was not impressed by the strength of the mighty; instinctively, I feared power and sympathized with the underdog.

The official Russian government immediately gave orders to open all businesses. Like bees from the hive, the Russian soldiers swarmed through the stores and bought everything they could lay their hands on. The storekeepers were curious: "Why do you Russians buy all the goods? Can't you buy them at home? Why do soldiers need nightgowns, babushkas, yard goods and ribbons?" "I want to send them to my wife and my parents. I want to show them that I love them and think about them. Hey! What do I see there on the shelf? Sell it to me."

"I can't sell you my whole store. Leave something for somebody else."

"Yes, you are right. We have everything in Russia."

From Russian soldiers who did not favor the Communist regime we learned that in Russia there was actually very little to buy. One of them said: "For 20 years we suffered from hunger, and there were few clothes to buy. For a pair of boots we have to save for years, because they cost 200 rubles; while here we can buy them for 20. For an egg, a little salt, sugar, meat or fish, we have to stand in long queues, and when we finally reach the store, often we find it is sold out."

A joke went around about the situation. A Jewish storekeeper asked a soldier on a shopping spree: "You can buy this in Russia, can't you?" "*Unas wsio yest.*" ("We have everything") replied the soldier. "Do you have *makes* and *tzores* (sores and aggravations)?" asked the shopkeeper. "*Unas wsio yest*" again was the answer of the soldier who, not knowing Yiddish, thought *makes* and *tzores* must be special goodies.

The Russian soldiers bought dozens of eggs and ate them

like vultures. The women of the Red army dressed themselves in silky nightgowns and, not knowing the difference, wore them as evening dresses to dances. Within a month, all the stores were closed again; everything was sold and new merchandise was not available. The Jewish people of our town, the majority of them storekeepers, were now idle.

With the Russian occupation, the population of eastern Poland became citizens of Russia. When our family received passports, each contained an 11th paragraph listing special restrictions for business people. We could not, for example, live in a large town within 100 kilometers from the borders. In addition we were constantly watched by the NKVD, the Russian political police, for anti-Soviet activities. Overnight we became poor people but, much worse, we became suspected people from whom the authorities never took their watchful eyes.

My older sister, Henia, left for Baranowicze before the Russian passports were issued. When she applied for her passport, she lied. She stated that her father was a common worker, a carpenter. By doing so she was the only one in the family who did not have the 11th paragraph in her passport. As a result, she was able to get a job in a canteen. My sister, Dalya, and I went back to school in Byten, by now converted to the White Russian system.

With lightning speed, the social and cultural life of our Jewish population in Byten was liquidated. All of the Jewish institutions, from the library to the charitable organizations, were disbanded. The Zionist groups stopped their activities. People who mentioned Zionism were sent to Siberia.

For a time, father was watchman in his own mill. At night he would fill his pockets with flour and barley to bring home. This was our sustenance. We had to share our house with two Russian women who were secretaries to the NKVD.

Once the Russians arrived, empty cattle trains began to

fill the rail yards in nearby Domanovo. They were to be used as transportation for people suspected of anti-Soviet activities. The secret police would surround the houses of suspects during the night and give them only a few minutes to collect the barest essentials. Nobody ever heard from them again. We learned later that they were taken to labor camps in Siberia.

We suffered terribly during the winter, not having money to buy firewood, and I found a way to get a little money for fuel. I sold some pieces of cut leather for sandals to one of the Russian secretaries who lived in our house. Later a member of the NKVD called me out of school and brought me to the police station for three hours of inter-rogation about my supposed connection with the black market:

"Don't you know that in Russia it is forbidden to engage in black market operations? Where do you buy and to whom do you sell the merchandise? I'll let you go free if you give me the names of the black marketeers. If not, you'll be sent to jail without seeing your parents."

"I didn't buy the leather to sell it. I had it before the war, but the shoemaker was too busy to make sandals for me. Our house is cold. I offered to sell the leather so we can buy firewood."

"You are a liar!"

In spite of the interrogator's scare tactics, I denied any in-volvement with the black market. He kept insisting. I was an anti-Soviet activist, he charged, a capitalist parasite. He shook his finger at me and said:

"We'll search your house. Your parents are industrialists, dirty capitalists. We know you are connected with the black market."

"Go ahead and do that," I said calmly, yet in mortal fear that, in their search, they would find the better clothing and few pieces of yard goods that father had hidden in the driedup well in the mill yard. (People of my father's generation remembered World War I when money had no value and farmers bartered their food for other merchandise.)

He let me sit there alone for half an hour. All kinds of thoughts wandered through my mind; I was sure I'd never see my parents again. He came back into the room to ask me the same questions and I denied them again and again. I think my composure convinced him I was telling the truth. Finally, in a milder tone, he told me to go home and never tinker with the black market.

Back at home, I asked the Russian secretary who lived with us why she had reported me. She told me that she had been so pleased with her purchase that she showed it to her employer's wife. She, in turn, told her husband, the chief of the secret police. The secretary was innocent and had never intended to do me any harm.

We observed that, in general, the moral standards of the Russian girls were quite different from ours. Many of them believed in free love. As soon as the girls gave birth to children they gave them to a government institution where they were raised. The girls had no responsibilities toward their babies. As the children grew up, they were regimented into a strict Communist environment, learning little if anything about western civilization.

On November 30, 1939, Russia invaded Finland, to round out the borders of her western defenses. She demanded from Finland territory to construct military installations. On March 12, 1940, the Finns surrendered. Later on, when the Germans attacked Leningrad, it became clear why Russia attacked Finland. Finland's added territory helped the Russians save Leningrad from German hands.

In Byten, meanwhile, the talk of forming collective farms was causing discontent among farmers. They began to realize they had been better off under the Polish government. The Soviet regime taxed them heavily, not in money but in kind. They had to deliver, live, a proportion of the cattle they owned and there was even a norm of potatoes to be given, according to average yield.

Farmers and town dwellers alike became more unhappy with their new master. People were afraid to voice their opinions because the secret police were everywhere. Even neighbors and relatives had been known to go to the police in moments of anger. At night, when the town was asleep, the police came and took the accused away.

To keep people from thinking and to gain the confidence of the youth of the town, the Russians arranged dances, propaganda films, political debates—all sorts of entertainment. Russian officers were excellent performers. They were superb dancers, sang beautifully and were effective public speakers. The moment the Russians occupied a village, they began staging pageantry and the young people devoured it.

If the Russians had implemented their regime in a gradual and peaceful manner, the people might have learned to accept them. The storekeepers and small manufacturers eventually would have become accustomed to being managers of state enterprises. Education was free, and if a student had good grades he was paid to go to college. But the activities of the secret police, the absence of civil courts, the uprooting of large segments of the population and their resettling in eastern Russia, and the substitution of Russians in our community were impossible to accept.

On April 9, 1940, Germany invaded Denmark and Norway. On May 10, a blitzkrieg attack was launched on France via the Netherlands, Belgium and Luxembourg. Hitler bottled up the Allied forces at Dunkirk (May 30–June 4). Italy declared war on France on June 10. Caught between the Germans and Italians, France capitulated on June 21.

The fall of France shocked us terribly. Hitler was now

the master of the mainland of Western Europe. We were in mortal fear that Germany might also turn against Russia and conquer it. What then would become of us Jews?

Part Three: The German occupation

3

In 1941, June 22 fell on a Sunday, a beautiful summer day. Not quite awake, I stretched lazily beneath the blanket of my bed. The chirping of birds on the plum tree near my window and the caressing rays of the rising sun made me forget momentarily the realities of life. A dim recollection of a better past floated in my mind. I felt safe, happy with normal adolescent fantasies. I was 16.

My daydreams ended abruptly. My father, returning from his morning prayers, announced that the Germans were at war with Russia. They had begun bombarding our villages and cities at 4 a.m. By noon, reconnaisance planes were over Byten, and airfields and railway stations in our vicinity were targets of bombs.

We noticed wildly erratic activities. Russian military trucks and cars sped eastward. Local Russian government authorities had fled during the night. Chaos prevailed in the streets. Some young men loaded their belongings on their bicycles and sped off with the retreating Russian army. They were sprayed by bullets from German aircraft and very few survived. Farmers came flocking into town, sacking the few Russian stores and warehouses. Nobody slept. We kept hearing rumors that our town was already surrounded by the Germans.

Tuesday we heard sporadic gunfire and saw splinters of

debris leap into the air. A Russian plane had been shot down over a meadow nearby.

In their haste to leave, the NKVD had left files behind. A local policeman who had seen the files told us that our family headed the list of people who were to be sent to Siberia. We knew, of course, we had nothing better to expect from the Germans. Either way, my parents kept saying, we were lost.

On Wednesday afternoon, a few minutes after a German patrol came walking down our main street, we heard machine gun fire from the Polish Catholic church. I saw a few retreating Russian soldiers shoot at the Germans, who managed to dodge the bullets and disappear. That evening, Byten was strafed by artillery as the Germans moved in to occupy it. Learning that the population was primarily Jewish, the soldiers started screaming that the Jews were the criminals who had brought on the war. Waves of German soldiers passed through Byten for 17 days. Finally, a local military government was established, headed by SS men. Their names were Weber, Shulke, Haniftal, Gotschlict, Hirshe, Schwartz, Gruber and Tschorchin.

The first government order concerned roads which, in the eastern part of Poland, were generally very bad. The road that led from Byten to Slonim was exceptionally sandy and hilly, too much of a challenge for some of the army trucks. One day in July, the Germans ordered 350 Jews to report at six the next morning to start fixing the roads. When less than 340 reported, German soldiers broke into Jewish homes and dragged out children, old people and even women breast-feeding their babies. My youngest brother, Chaim, though only 12, was one of those dragged off to work.

Every day the Germans came up with new demands for us to meet. They asked that we Jews form a *Judenrath,* a body of people who would represent the entire Jewish population of our town. They also ordered the Jews to turn in fur coats, jewelry, precious metals, cloth, flour and large amounts of money. Then they ransacked homes for remaining possessions.

We soon heard rumors that Jews living in the neighboring shtetls had been murdered. The word was that the marching German soldiers were taking as many Jews as they could, dragging them to the outskirts of their towns and shooting them.

In August, the local White Russian police were organized under the name "Samochova" and a Polish shoemaker, Kibinsky, a habitual drunk, was placed in charge. It was he who delivered the German order that all Jews wear a wide white band with a yellow Star of David on their upper left arms. Any Jew who left the house without the Star of David sign would be immediately shot down. There was great confusion in Byten as everybody began looking for yellow material or thread to embroider the yellow star. There simply wasn't enough yellow material to be found. For the first few days nobody left home except to go on forced labor.

If we felt shame before the Germans we were ashamed more before the local Polish and White Russian population. It was hard to get used to the mocking of our neighbors, but we slowly learned to swallow the acts of degradation. Our only prayer was that we would live through the war and that the future would hold better promise for us. But this looked unlikely. By autumn of 1941, the Germans had taken over White Russia and most of the Ukraine. In the north, Leningrad was in a state of siege; in the south, the Germans had entered the Crimean Peninsula and were besieging Sebastopol; and on the central front they were within 25 miles of Moscow.

In our town, the entire Jewish population, except for the sick and the very old, was divided into work groups. Every evening the *Judenrath* issued orders for the next day. Some groups were designated to chop firewood, some to clean the

German horses and buggies and some to clean the German barracks and wash the soldiers' clothes.

My sisters, brother and I went to work every day: Henia at the SS headquarters (in the new school building), washing floors and shining the officers' boots; Dalya in a lumber mill eight kilometers away. Sometimes, when there was a shortage of manpower, they also made my father work, as they did my married sister, Yentl, mother of a five-year-old daughter and pregnant with another child.

My brother and I walked seven kilometers every day to the railway station at Domanovo to load and unload logs and freight, as well as chop wood, wash floors and carry water. Often we were beaten by German soldiers on their way to the front. Our yellow stars seemed to goad them into acts of terror.

For a time I worked in the garden of an SS man. In the morning I polished his boots, brought in the firewood and later joined some of my people who were weeding the vegetable garden. One day the SS man came out to talk to us. He was young, good looking and seemed friendly. He told us that in Germany he was studying philosophy. Finally, I asked, "Can you explain why such educated people as the Germans became murderers? You know how they treat us, that they kill us?"

"We follow orders from the Fuhrer; we are engaged in a war."

"But you are a philosophy student! Surely you understand that you cannot follow orders blindly. Not when the orders are to commit murder. Where is your conscience? That is the difference between the animals and man. We all have to live with our conscience."

With his polished boot and with all his force, the officer kicked me in my stomach. Knocked to the ground, I saw stars in my eyes and I couldn't get up.

"You swine, *farfluchter Jude*, I should shoot you on the spot, the way you talk about us Germans! But maybe it is the conscience you talk about that prevents me!" With that, he turned and went back to the house, slamming the door behind him.

I couldn't walk back home; my friends carried me most of the way. The doctor in the ghetto thought that I was bleeding internally. To this day, I have pains in my right side, and to this incident I attribute my not being able to bear children. Yet I was lucky in a way; many Jews were killed for lesser crimes.

We worked hard, believing that the Germans would let us live as long as we could produce and be useful to them. The *Judenrath* constantly bribed the local authorities to keep them friendly, but they could not prevent new indignities. Now we were required to wear yellow Stars of David on both our backs and chests. We had to wear them even at home.

There was another ominous development one Tuesday evening in September, 1941. Some 200 Lithuanian soldiers, under the command of a German SS lieutenant, marched into town. The lieutenant ordered the *Judenrath* to deliver, within 30 minutes, 130 different items in specified quantities. I remember only a few of them: cigarettes, 150 packs of tobacco, rubber boots, officer's boots, stockings, underwear, towels, blankets, matches, soap and two and a half kilograms of gold.

The Jews deposited their valuables before the SS headquarters, but it was not enough. Every Jewish home was now vulnerable to ransacking by the Lithuanians. Our fear was indescribable, especially when we heard what these Lithuanians had done the day before in Zyrowice, 18 kilometers away. They had lined up all the Jews around the famous Jesuit monastery and then ordered them to take shovels and dig their own graves. They gunned them down. Local residents tried to persuade them to let two Jews live—the only doctor in the vicinity and another man they deemed indispensable. The Lithuanians finally gave in to the demands of the people, but refused to spare the families of the two men. Both men chose to die rather than be separated from their dear ones.

The holocaust was moving closer. We learned that the Lithuanians had been ordered to kill 500 men from our community, but had been persuaded by local SS authorities to postpone the massacre because help was needed to clear the heavy snows from the highways. After two days of terrorizing, the Lithuanians left Byten to proceed with their exterminations in other Jewish communities.

Gradually we came to accept the idea that any minute might be our last. Resigned to this fate we started to breathe a little easier. But the picture of a mass grave was impossible to erase from our minds. Parents cried bitterly because their children never smiled anymore. Their sad eyes stared from the hollows of their bony faces. They were emaciated, dirty and always whimpering. Even the youngest seemed to realize that they might soon be thrown into graves and covered by the ugly earth.

On Friday, November 14 1941, some farmers returned to Byten and reported they had not been allowed to enter Slonim. White Russian police and German solders blockaded the city. A few days later we found out why. On November 14, the ghetto in Slonim (25,000 Jews) had undergone its first liquidation. Under the leadership of the county commissar—a known sadist and murderer—German soldiers, along with the local White Russian police and the corps of Lithuanians, had gone from house to house rounding up Jews. They searched the crawl spaces, cellars and attics. When they found their prey, they loaded them on trucks and hauled them to an immense pit dug by farmers from another village. Forced to undress completely, the Jews were marched into the pit and machine-gunned. They formed a mountain of corpses as they fell. Some who were merely wounded suffocated under the weight of the dead bodies that fell on top of them.

A few of the wounded, who happened to be in the upper layers of the mass grave, crawled out during the night. Dressed in rags they were able to beg in the nearest village, they were smuggled back into the ghetto, but not for long. Authorities, learning of the escape, came back to the ghetto and demanded that the few survivors be turned over to them immediately. They were brought back to the same grave and shot again.

Some 9,400 Jews were killed between 7 a.m. and 5 p.m. Thus the Jewish community of Slonim, for generations the social and cultural center for smaller Jewish communities surrounding it, lost in one day 40 percent of its people.

Details of the Slonim massacre came primarily from a young Gentile who often undertook to deliver messages and news from one town to another. He was paid for his work but he risked his life for us and we admired him. His voice shook with disgust as he told us that, after the Germans had taken the most valuable possessions, the people of Slonim and the farmers from the surrounding area flocked into the ghetto and looted it. They swarmed through the homes, taking away furniture, pillows, blankets, clothing and anything else they could carry. They were ecstatic because of the unexpected generosity of the Germans in sharing their spoils.

December, 1941, was another dark month. Some SS troops—trained murderers and shrewd in their cruelties—came to Byten. They immediately took over the biggest house in town. After painting the house and furnishing it with the best of furniture and linen, they began harrassing our people. Within three days they had killed six refugees from western Poland who were trying to find sanctuary in Byten.

Even the elements were harsh. The winter of 1941-42 was exceptionally cold. In temperatures that often dropped to 40 degrees below zero we worked from sunrise to sunset shoveling snow to keep the highway open. When we were finally allowed to go home we walked in a trance. The next morning, after little or no sleep, the drudgery would begin again.

December 20 brought another ultimatum from the Germans. We were to deliver to them 200,000 Russian rubles, two kilograms of gold, yard goods, fur, jewelry and leather. There was panic as we tried to figure out where to get what they wanted. At the home of Rabbi Lieberman we deposited what was left of our meager belongings. With tears in their eyes, women parted with wedding rings, gold chains, watches, silverware and possessions they had inherited from their parents, who had also inherited them. The dentists were busy pulling out gold teeth. To raise the 200,000 rubles we had to sell the last of our cloth to farmers. Meanwhile, most members of our *Judenrath* were held in Slonim as hostages. After seven days we delivered their ransom.

Barely clothed, cold, always hungry, worn out from hard work and psychologically exhausted from constant torment, we could feel our will to live being slowly drained from us.

Some 120 young men, among them my brother-in-law, Lejba, were taken to a labor camp 20 kilometers from Slonim to build a new highway. I remember the lamentations of my sister, Yentl, and of my parents when Lejba left. No one believed we would ever see him again.

But there were hopeful signs, also. It became clear that the Germans were not prepared to fight in the bitter Russian winter and did not calculate such heavy Russian resistance. A counter-offensive, launched by the Russians in the winter of 1941-42, saved Moscow. While the Germans vented their frustrations on us, the Jews, our prospects for survival seemed slightly better. Defeat for Germany was possible.

For evidence we had only to look at German soldiers returning to Germany. Covered with lice, wearing dirty, torn uniforms, their rosy cheeks frostbitten, they were dejected and depressed. They were no longer singing *Deutschland, Deutschland Uber Alles*. They were grateful for a single pair of woolen socks, which our farm women were obliged to knit for them. Once we had been almost convinced of the superiority of the German soldiers—so well-dressed, clean-cut and confident they were. It was not without satisfaction that we now viewed the shattered examples of the "superior race." Some of the soldiers even voiced the opinion that history would repeat itself—that the German army would suffer the same fate as Napoleon's army in its war with Russia.

In March, 1942, a development in the town of Iwacewicze would directly affect our life in Byten. All 600 Jews in that community were banished. Taking with them only what they could carry, they were led to the woods and told to go where they pleased. In stormy, sub-zero weather, they wandered through the forest. That night 21 Jews froze to death.

When a few members of the group reached Byten, the Jewish committee hired horses and buggies to pick up others still scattered in the fields and woods. Every Jewish family in Byten had to take in one family. For those too poor to feed a refugee family, a food collection was organized. Our Jewish population was only 1,000 and we suddenly had on our hands an additional burden of 400 people, but none of us complained. We shared the little we had. The *Judenrath* even appealed to Jews remaining in the Slonim ghetto and, in a few days, two wagonloads of food and clothing were received from Slonim for distribution. By July, 200 of our friends from Iwacewicze were allowed to return to their homes, only to be massacred in a later liquidation of their ghetto.

4

Rumors began reaching us in May, 1942, that a partisan movement was being organized in the surrounding woods. Groups of partisans would attack Germans who passed through desolate areas, taking away their weapons and killing them. Although the rumors of their deeds had a legendary flavor, they proved to be true. During that month, partisans swept into the village where my brother-in-law was held. They took food, horses and carriages from the farmers and moved in on the forced-labor camp. As the White Russian guards fled, the partisans flung the camp doors open, freeing the Jews.

Great was our joy when Lejba came home. His little daughter, Rochele, six years old, climbed up on his lap, hugging and kissing him and crying, "I thought I lost you for good." His son, Matys, whom we had nicknamed Memele was only six months old, but in his own way he felt our happiness in being together again. His sky-blue eyes sparkled even thought he was half-starved.

By this time, the Jews of Byten were confined within the barbed-wire boundaries of the ghetto. The ghetto consisted of 48 small wooden houses for 1,200 people. As many as 20 lived in a single room. To make more sleeping room, the houses were emptied of furniture. The kitchen and yard were available for cooking, but there was very little cooking to do. Each person received 25 dekagrams (four ounces) of black bread a day. People who could afford a barley soup or a little buckeye flour were greatly envied. From a charitable committee in the ghetto, the very poor could get a little cereal or flour from time to time.

To make it easier for youngsters to bear their hunger, the children were sent to a school, which was conducted in yards and gardens. Even at the tender age of five, children had a true understanding of the prayer, *"Maayin yovoh ezri"* ("From where my help will come").

Our whole family—including Yentl, her husband and their two children—were put in one room in a house. No larger than 10 feet by 12, it was simply not big enough, so father, Henia, Dalya and I slept in the barn. From our window, we could see the Jewish cemetery about a kilometer away. My father would look out that window and murmur, "How I envy the peace of the dead! How lucky they are to have a resting place at last!" Every morning, Henia asked my father to open the prayer book at random to see if that page had in it any consolation, any indication of hope.

My father had always been a slight man; now he looked worse than a corpse. His flesh was thin with a leathery texture and a yellow color. His lifeless blue eyes were sunk deep in his blackened eye sockets.

My mother would send me to call father home for a little hot soup that looked like mud. It consisted of some buckwheat flour in boiled water. Father would refuse to eat it and gave his soup to Chaim. He was ready to die, he said, but he wanted his children to survive.

Whenever my sisters or I were sent to work on the highways around meadows or woods, we would pick a few spinach leaves or berries to smuggle back into the ghetto. Once I jeopardized my life trying to get food. It happened when I was working at the railway station in Domanovo. I left the labor crew, walked to the local miller and asked for flour. He knew that we had been millers, too, before the war and was sympathetic. I hid until evening and joined my work group on their way home, concealing four kilograms of flour. All the seven kilometers my teeth didn't stop chattering. I could not control my fear of being caught by the police or the SS. Fortunately, I was not caught.

My kid brother, Chaim, also worked in this group, loading and unloading the freight cars. One day on our way home, he said, "Don't tell the others, but I was beaten up today by some soldiers on their way to the front. They saw the yellow star on my back and started to ridicule me: 'Do you work hard, Jew boy? How old are you? Come kiss my ass. I'll give you a taste of the war.' A young soldier started pulling my ears, saying, 'Because of you Jews we have to fight a war. You are all communists and want to dominate the world.' Then he kicked me and beat me over the head. I just don't have an appetite today."

He handed me his crusty slice of bread, the daily ration of each working person and said, "Here, you eat it."

Now, 33 years later, whenever I think of my brother, I see those outstretched, calloused hands of his, giving me his only food.

My heart cries out for him and all the innocent Jewish children who were victimized by the sadistic side of human nature. Those children had no youth; they suffered hunger, beatings, hard labor and agonizing death. No words can describe the remorse I feel when I think of my brother's kindness and the kindness he felt for others in spite of the hatred he received.

Hitler, in the summer of 1942, shifted his main attack to the south, directing an offensive against the oil fields of the Caucasus. Sevastopol soon fell, and the siege of Stalingrad began. The Germans were within a hundred miles of the Caspian Sea.

Nearer home, the Germans opened a large ammunition factory in Slonim and Jews from the Slonim ghetto were part of the work force. With ingenuity they were able to smuggle out military hardware for partisan units in the area.

On June 29, 1942, the ghetto in Slonim went through another liquidation. We learned of the details during the first days of July. This liquidation was no different from the others: first the ghetto had been blockaded; next the victims were taken in big trucks to the outskirts of town where gaping holes were ready for them; then they were shot.

Many Jews had tried to prepare for this day by digging hiding places under their vegetable gardens. The Germans knew this but were unable to find these havens during the short hours of the liquidation. So they set fire to the ghetto, burning alive many hundreds of Jews in their hiding places. Those who did come out leaped with their clothes flaming into the Szczara River.

There was more terror to come. On the banks of the same river stood a maternity hospital. The SS troopers marched into the hospital, grabbed the infants by their feet, spread their legs until they were split in half and threw them through the windows into the river. That Friday the water of the river was red with the blood of Jewish infants. The mothers were shot in their beds. Later their bodies were burned in the inferno.

We in Byten knew that we were next in line. Diligently we prepared hiding places in the barns, cellars, caves, vegetable gardens and in the double floors and double roofs of the attics.

Father flatly informed us that he was not going to hide, that he would be the first to come out, for he welcomed death. Mother kept telling us that we should try our best to hide from our murderers, that, should we survive the war, we could join our brother or her brother and sisters in America.

Mother by now was quite ill and bothered by dizzy spells. She had been a heavy woman, about 180 pounds, and now she was only skin and bones. She had even shrunk

in height and could hardly drag her feet. To the last
minute, however, she tried to carry the yoke of the family.
She would stand near the barbed wire and plead with passing farmers to bring her some flour or a little milk for her
infant granddaughter in exchange for a dress, suit or a
shirt. We children were so frightened that we accused her
of not caring for our safety. Had the police caught her ex-
changing goods with the farmers, they would have killed
her and the entire family.

Our White Russian neighbors were no more merciful
than the German guards. For an egg or a little piece of
cheese or a bite of bread, they took our last pieces of
clothing. We were going to be killed anyway, they said; we
would have no use for clothing.

The slightest movement of police or military frightened
us. On the first Saturday in July, cars with White Russian
police came to our town to look for partisans; we were sure
they had come to kill us. Every house in the ghetto elected
someone to stand guard and give an alarm if they saw
police surround our ghetto.

Friday, July 24, 1942, was the day after *Tisha B'av*, during which everybody had fasted. The young people had
left the ghetto to work with their groups, and the older ones
were sitting in the yards under the shade of the trees, for it
was very hot. Those who still had a little barley and beans
prepared the *cholents* for the Sabbath—*Sabbath Nachamu*,
the sabbath of consolation and comfort.

When the workers returned they brought news that the
local police had gathered farmers from three nearby
villages and were forcing them to dig pits. The panic in the
ghetto was overpowering. Each family inspected its hiding
place. Rabbi Jaffe and Rabbi Lieberman conducted Friday
night services, as usual, and chanted the part of the Torah
that says, *"Nachamu, machamu, ami"* ("Be comforted my
people"). Suddenly several young men burst in, agitation
reflected in their faces. They told the congregation to go

home and prepare their hiding places. Our ghetto had been scheduled for liquidation.

5

Everybody slept fully clothed that night. As usual, father, Chaim and I were stretched out on straw sacks in the barn. Henia stood watch. At 3 a.m., she woke us up. "I hear walking and running in the yards," she said. Leaving the barn we saw that the whole ghetto had been aroused; it was surrounded by police.

In our barn there was a hiding place for about 10 people, camouflaged with firewood. My brother-in-law grabbed Yentl and their two children and forced them into it in spite of the objections of others that there was not enough room. He put back the lid of the hiding place and threw firewood over it. He himself had no chance to hide; German police and Lithuanians were already inside the ghetto. He ran for cover between the vegetable beds where he was discovered by a gendarme and shot. Lejba was the first in the ghetto to be killed.

My father refused to hide. In his sheepskin jacket he stood in the doorway of the house like a corpse—his face the color of river mud, his eyes unfocused. On that hot summer day of July 25 he shivered with cold, waiting to be delivered from the shackles of the tormenting life of the ghetto.

Mother, Henia, Dalya, Chaim and I climbed to the attic, where 15 people were already hiding. In the attic, we had stored Passover pots, pans and dishes, all covered with rags. Henia came over and told me to lie down among the dishes in the narrow space where the roof touched the walls. I did, and she covered me with rags. She herself was highly sensitive and confinement nauseated her. Unwilling to cover herself up, she, mother and Chaim watched from an attic window and saw people being dragged from their homes, gardens and hiding places. They were clubbed over the heads and forced to climb into trucks formerly used for cattle. They saw father being led to one of the trucks.

After 20 minutes we heard knocking on the lid door to the attic. Local policemen climbed the stairs to corral anybody they found hiding there. I heard Henia begging one policeman, whom she knew by name, to leave her in the attic; she promised to give him money and jewelry. He asked for it immediately, but she told him she had it hidden in the ghetto. She promised to give it to him as soon as things quieted down. He dragged her down the stairs by her hair.

The police failed to look where I lay hidden under the rags, paralyzed with fear and shock. I listened to the machine guns and prayed that my mother, father, sisters and brother would have easy deaths. (I was so shocked that I lost forever the memory of their faces. In 1947, when I arrived in the United States, I found at my brother's house an old picture of my family. In this picture I was about four years old. Now, I remember my lost family only by that picture. In nightmares I am always hunted by murderers; as I run from them in fields, woods and mud, I am with my family, but I never see their faces.)

After the shooting stopped, I could hear horses and carriages in the ghetto and the voices of our White Russian neighbors who came to loot. They dug up nearly every foot of earth looking for buried treasures. Like wild animals over their prey, our Gentile neighbors threw themselves on the loot.

As it grew dark a deathly silence prevailed. Suddenly I heard a voice reciting psalms. I looked out and saw a very old man with a long white beard praying and crying. Then, miraculously, I saw my sister, Dalya, crawling out of her hiding place. I had been sure she was taken away with the others. I kept embracing her to convince myself I wasn't dreaming. She told me that at the last minute Henia pushed her down in the crawl space among the dishes. Because of Henia both of us were alive; she had looked out for everybody but herself.

Dalya and I decided to see if anybody else had survived the liquidation. Descending from the attic we heard one of my girlfriends calling loudly, "Is anybody alive in this house? Come down, the massacre is over." We were terribly hungry and in the hearth we found the *cholent* that had been prepared for the day before. We devoured it greedily and then ran to Yentl's hiding place.

We heard a baby's cry and some voices. As I started to take away the firewood stacked on top, the sounds ceased. Finally I saw the lid of the hiding place and drew it open. It was dark inside, with a single ray of light coming in from an air hole at the top. I called into the darkness. Among the dozen people who crawled out I saw my sister, Yentl, and her children. It was the baby's cries that I had heard.

The Germans had also heard the baby's cries, but were not exactly sure where the noise was coming from. Also they didn't have time to remove the firewood. Yentl said that, at first, Henia had joined her in the hiding place. She left, knowing the stale air underground would make her ill. She then joined the rest of us in the attic, from which she was taken and put to death.

Later we learned that six trucks of police and one carload of Germans from Slonim, together with the gendarmes from Byten and our local White Russian police, had carried out the mission of liquidation. They had loaded 840 Jews on cattle trucks and beat them on the head to confuse them and prevent their resistance. The Jews were then driven to a big hole, where they were ordered to undress and lie down. They were machine-gunned from above.

Farmers from neighboring villages greedily hauled the clothes away, but not until the Germans searched pockets and linings for hidden diamonds or gold. The grave was covered with just a few shovelsful of dirt but the earth at the site wouldn't stop shaking. The pressure of blood oozing from the pit split the ground.

Monday morning was inventory time. Four gendarmes came to the ghetto to make a head-count. There were now 340 of us. We were told we had one month to live. They ordered us to move to the synagogue and the 10 small houses near it. Each day thereafter, the gendarmes dragged us to work, making us clean up the depopulated ghetto. Farmers still came to look for hidden treasure. Whatever we found we tried to destroy so our enemies could not benefit from it.

From time to time we overheard farmers discussing the activities of the partisans. Apparently they were making an effort to weaken the Germans and local police by attacking their headquarters in nearby villages. It became clear to us that our only choice was to run away to the woods and join the partisans before the Germans had a chance to finish us off. We discovered that Jews from surrounding cities had already joined the movement in a forest called Wolcze Nory (wolves' nests).

Beginning to fear the partisans, the Germans in Byten were now dragging us out every day to dig trenches around the city. Although the police stood watch every night, a dozen young men succeeded in leaving the ghetto for the Wolcze Nory. A farmer who helped them make contact with the partisans paid dearly for his deed. He and his entire family were brutally murdered by the Germans.

With our young men escaping, some of the Jews feared

the Germans would kill us all. These people tried to in-
fluence the young people not to leave. We who planned to
go became more secretive.

Yentl, with her small children, and Dalya, who was 19,
and I, 17, were especially vulnerable because we were
without any male protection. But I was determined not to
be led to death like a little lamb. No matter what the consequences, I decided to flee to the woods. Since I would not
dream of leaving my two sisters, niece and nephew behind,
I started to condition them for an escape. I told them to be
ready to leave at a second's notice. Sleeping little, I snooped
around trying to find out when the next party would leave.

Thursday, August 13, when I returned from forced
labor, I learned that 50 tradespeople who worked directly
for the gendarmes had left the ghetto. They went away
with the gendarmes who assured them they had their full
protection. The guards even allowed them to remove their
yellow badges.

We who remained were convinced we were doomed,
that the Germans would surely kill us the next day. That
night I didn't sleep at all. I told my sisters to pack only
essentials,like milk and diapers for the baby, and to stay
awake. I left the house, looking for any movement. Around
midnight I heard voices coming from a barn on the banks of
a nearby stream. Beyond the stream lay meadows and grain
fields. Slipping into the barn, I saw a group of people ready
with their rucksacks to make their escape. I ran home and
gathered the family. The group tried to dissuade us from
joining them, telling us it would be impossible to escape
with an infant whose cries would alert the police. I said we
were going whether they liked it or not. In front of us, the
group held a conference and finally consented to our
coming, mainly because they were afraid of the commotion
we would have made had they refused.

About 100 people were gathered in the barn. They had
decided to divide up in groups of 10 or 12. The first group

cut the barbed wire and crawled through the stream to the high stand of grain. They disappeared into the darkness. After 10 minutes and no shooting, the coast was clear for the next group. But now we were no longer interested in order. We all started crawling through the foliage near the stream. Yentl, with her baby sucking at her breast to keep him quiet, fell into the water. When she shouted for help, I ran back, lifted her by the hand and took the package of diapers she was carrying, so she could run more easily. I told Rochele to hold on to her mother's coat. Dalya held on to Rochele's other hand.

Our problem now was not to lose the others in the group. I ran ahead, trying to keep contact with the man in front of us. Whenever my sisters lost sight of me they had to call my name; by the direction of my answer, they knew where to turn. A mile from the ghetto, we all regrouped to see if anyone was missing. Suddenly we heard the shooting of light rockets, and it seemed like daylight. The rockets came from the direction of the Jewish cemetery where the local police stood watch. Evidently they heard the commotion and began shooting. We fell flat on the ground. When it was dark and quiet again, I told my sisters to leave their rucksacks behind; it would be easier for them to run. I kept my package not only because I was stronger but because the fear in me generated enough energy to enable me to carry a small mountain.

Stealthily we crossed the Domanovo highway. By this time the children were tired but, understanding the danger we were in, they behaved like grownups. Life in the ghetto, with its hunger and fear, had hardened and matured them. At last we were able to rest. Near the village of Kochanowo we sat down in barley fields full of heavy, waving grain. With the sun about to rise, we began moving again. We reached the outskirts of the woods with the last of our strength.

Suddenly we spotted two dark figures moving among the

trees. We panicked, thinking the police had caught up with us. Happily, they turned out to be our people, young men who had escaped to the woods after the massacre. They undertook to be our guides and lead us to the partisans. Our spirits high, we lay down on the wet moss and drank water from the puddles. We picked wild berries and ate some hard bread we had taken from the ghetto.

Part Four: The partisans

6

Wolcze Nory was a stretch of fertile land in the midst of a thick forest, roughly 10 by 20 miles in area. It had been parceled off among five or six hundred peasants who, compared to peasants in surrounding villages, led healthy, prosperous lives.

When we arrived, we found the partisans gathered in the War Commission office, an unfinished building without doors or windows. In the group were people who escaped earlier from Byten as well as Jews from Slonim, Kosov and Iwacewicze. They surrounded us, asking questions: what was happening in the ghetto? who remained there still? what was their situation?

As we talked, Russian partisan groups passed the building, returning from their operations of the day. Their horsedrawn carriages were loaded with sacks of potatoes, loaves of bread and canisters of milk; pigs and cows were tied behind. Some of the Russian partisans wore Red army uniforms, but most were dressed as peasants, except that they carried rifles and guns, wore cartridge belts across their chests and had grenades hanging from their belts. One of them, seeing Yentl with her suckling son in her arms, handed her a pot of milk and a loaf of bread. It was like being in a different country, not on Germany territory. Our fears began to dissipate.

In a barn we found some straw and spread it on the floor so we could rest our weary bodies. Early the next morning one of the officers paid us a visit. A tall Ukranian with unruly bangs that covered most of his face, he carried a machine gun, had a revolver in his pocket and wore the inevitable cartridge belts. He stood before us and lectured us in his native tongue. He said that if our intentions were only to escape the German massacres, there was no place for us here; but if we had come to fight the Germans and revenge the spilt blood of our brethren, the partisans would help us organize and together we would fight our mutual enemy. He rebuked us for coming to the woods without arms: "Without arms, it is impossible to carry on partisan work." He told us we should try to buy weapons from farmers. One of our men who brought with him a spare pair of new boots made a connection with a local peasant and exchanged the boots for a machine gun. The next day the partisans gave us six rifles for the machine gun.

The forest was divided like a city into blocks with narrow footpaths and dirt roads running east and west, north and south. Each division, approximately half a square mile in area, contained a partisan group of 50 or 60 people. Each group had its own commanding officer and leaders. One was a political officer called the *politruk*, a Communist Party member whose task was to enlighten the partisans concerning communist ideology and to supervise the social life. Another was the administrative officer who was responsible for procuring food.

In effect, the partisans tweaked the tail of the German lion. The forest was a Communist stronghold in the midst of the German occupation. In addition there were many independent partisan divisions in other forests in the eastern part of Poland, in the Polish and Russian Ukraine and in the woods that cut through White Russian territory to Moscow. Each division kept in close touch with others in the various forests. They exchanged military information and received orders directly from the Red army. Later on, in 1944, the partisans built their own airfields in the woods, enabling Russian planes to land with special orders from Moscow. It was paradoxical that, while the Germans were at the gates of the Russian capital, a Communist regime was at their rear, ruling the woods and villages.

We who escaped from Byten made our camp about three miles from Wolcze Nory on hilly and heavily wooded land. The first day we were shown how to build huts. We cut flexible twigs and bent them in a half circle. After firmly sticking the ends of the twigs in the soft ground, we braided more twigs for the top and sides. For the roof we peeled bark off the trees. Later we brought straw and spread it inside to protect against the dampness of the earth.

Men of our group went to neighboring villages and brought back food and utensils so we could start a communal kitchen. They also brought two milking cows to provide fresh milk for the children. Not always did the farmer give us food of his own free will. Often he did so because he feared our guns as well as our membership in the strong partisan movement.

Each day more and more groups of Jews came to the woods. Most of them came from Slonim, Kosov, Iwacewicze and Byten. With the group from Iwacewicze came a child from our group who had been lost in the woods. The six-year-old told us that she had fallen into a swamp and had not been able to get up. A few hours later, seeing people walk through the woods, she managed to drag herself out of the mud and follow them unnoticed. In the morning one of the Byten Jews recognized her and brought her to our camp.

Adjacent to our camp was Group 51, the pride of the partisan movement. Jews from Slonim, numbering about a hundred, they were all young men and heavily armed.

Most of them had been employed by the Germans, sorting out weapons. It was they who smuggled military supplies to the partisans.

Group 58, the partisan group from Kosov, numbered more than 200. When the Russian partisans attacked their city, they asked the Jews to join them. The Kosov Jews brought with them guns, sewing machines, cobbler equipment, yard goods and any other useful materials they could put in their wagons. In the woods they set up trade shops that served all the partisans. The tailoring department sewed and mended clothes. The locksmiths tried to build cannons from parts of abandoned tanks.

We were Group 60. There were 200 of us and we were allotted the housekeeping chores. We worked in the communal kitchen, which served hot meals twice a day. We gathered firewood and made the fires, peeled potatoes and washed dishes. Women worked in the laundry, mended clothes and went to the fields every day to dig potatoes. Toward the end of the day, men loaded the sacks of potatoes and brought them to camp where they were stored underground for the winter.

One day, as we dug for potatoes, we suddenly heard gunfire and saw bullets overhead. Looking up I saw mounted police riding toward us. We all ran to the woods, but I was too far away to make it to cover. Seeing clusters of bushes in the middle of the field I crawled between the branches. I held my breath as the horsemen moved past me, but I was not noticed. After more shooting, the police left. They were a small group and did not dare enter the partisan stronghold. I ran back to the woods but lost my orientation; I did not find my group again until the next day. Luckily, no one had been killed.

It was difficult for us to come to terms with our new environment. The straw underneath didn't really keep us dry as we slept and we were covered by huge, white field-lice. They crawled into our long hair, which we couldn't cut for lack of scissors. We found it difficult to sleep nights because, though we were fully clothed, the lice managed to crawl all over us and bite us. Every night we made a fire, took off our clothes and held them above the flame until the heat made the lice drop into the fire. But it was a losing battle. As soon as we lay down, we were again covered with them.

My sister, Yentl, found the life particularly harsh. By nature delicate and sensitive, she could not even eat the food from the communal kitchen. Because she did not eat, she had no milk in her breasts for her son. The hungry baby sucked so hard that she would scream with pain. The lice made her break out in huge boils on her shoulders, her breasts and her feet. Yentl cried and blamed me for bringing her to the woods: "Bryna, you're responsible for my misery. It would have been easier to be killed by the Germans in the ghetto. We'll not survive the war—I nor my children. So why suffer? In the ghetto death comes quickly; in the ghetto you do not die alone, the community dies with you. Why should I live without my husband? My parents and so many who are dear to me have been liquidated." I would try to comfort her, to convince her to weather the hard times. "After the storm, good weather comes," I said. "You *do* have a reason to live—you have your son and daughter."

"No, we are all doomed. Look at Rochele. I can't shield her from her fright, from her longing for her dead father, from her fear that she might lose me, too. All the children in the woods are wise beyond their years. They don't cry, they don't ask for anything. The childish smiles have disappeared; their faces are lined with knowledge and cares that children should not have."

My heart ached as I listened to Yentl. We were victims and, to victims, there is precious little hope—only the constant pressure of deprivation. Yet, my mouth uttered words my mind refused to believe: "Yentl, dear, tomorrow may be a better day. The war may not last long."

By this time, our Group 60 numbered 370 Jews who had escaped from the Byten, Iwacewicze and Kosov ghettos. With us were six infants and 24 children. We organized a kindergarten and taught them songs and dances to make them forget, at least for a short time, the nightmare of their young lives. Little by little their sad eyes regained their natural sparkle. They played games lightheartedly, no longer cramped by the barbed-wire ghetto.

Unfortunately, the kindergarten in Wolcze Nory didn't last long. Nazi tormentors finally reached the woods. Barely six weeks after we arrived, reports began to reach us of renewed military activities on the roads and in the villages. A mood of doom and gloom deepened in our group as we realized that peril was again imminent.

In the fall of 1942, massive German forces began an all-out assault on Stalingrad, the vital key to all transport on the lower Volga. By November the Germans penetrated the city but Russian soldiers and the civilian population took a desperate stand. After weeks of house-to-house fighting, the Russians began a counterattack under General Zhukov. Twenty-two German divisions were forced to capitulate, and more than 330,000 Germans were lost in the epic battle at Stalingrad. As the Russians pushed westward, the Germans, wanting to keep the railways and highways free of sabotage, started an intensive campaign against the partisans.

The partisan groups among us who were better armed left our woods. Attacking and overpowering small German posts, they reached the Pinsker woods with barely a casualty. There they were safe from the Germans, for the woods and marshes stretched deep into Russia, almost to Moscow itself. Whenever the Germans tried to fight them, the partisans merely moved deeper into the woods. Compared to the Pinsker woods, our Wolcze Nory looked like a park. The Germans would have no trouble ambushing us!

Our Group 60, with its many women, children and old people, was now called *"Semejner lager,"* the family group. Still, the partisan chief of staff sent us a Russian to instruct us in the use of weapons and a Russian supervisor named Seryosha who was our political leader.

More recent escapees from Byten told us the situation was so horrible that even the gendarmes had expressed pity.

As we later learned, the Byten Jews found an end to their suffering on August 29, 1942. At four o'clock that Saturday morning, the ghetto was surrounded by Lithuanians, who were stationed in Byten to give "protection to the city against the partisans." They entered the homes of the remaining inhabitants, dragged them out of their hiding places, clubbing them over the heads. Herding them in front of a Jewish home, they ordered the Jews to sit motionless in the street. They sat without moving until 10 a.m., by which time the murderers had found every last one of the 140 remaining Jews. They marched them down Church Street to the grave that contained the first 840. A man who had owned a liquor store before the war tried to run away and hid in the bushes. The gendarmes shot him down as he fled. On command, the Jews took off their clothes and lay down in the grave. A volley of bullets penetrated their convulsive bodies. The dead and the wounded were then covered with earth still soaked with blood of the victims of the first liquidation. Before they fired, the gendarmes took the best of the clothes. The rest were left for the farmers.

We received the news of the second liquidation with indifference. We had become conditioned to the idea that we were all marked for death. We had escaped into the woods but we gave ourselves little chance to survive the war. We only hoped that when our time came, we would die taking vengeance for the spilled Jewish blood.

Soon it was decided that our group would be subdivided according to military tasks. Two departments would be responsible for sabotaging the enemy and providing food for the entire group. The third department was to keep careful watch over the woods. Guard posts were set up in all the camps and on the outskirts of the woods. At any indication of suspicious activity or sign of danger, we were to fire three shots to warn the other partisans. I was the only girl in our camp who was assigned to guard duty. Every day I stood guard for eight hours.

7

The clouds that had been gathering over us finally broke into a torrential hell. We heard shooting in the woods and learned that we were surrounded. German ambushes made many roads impassable. But the Wolcze Nory chief of staff remained calm. He assured us that we were invulnerable, that the German army would not dare to penetrate a strong partisan fortress. However, he did take some extra precautions—increasing patrols, ordering us to fell trees and barricade the larger roads. Huge trees, hundreds of years old, lined both sides of the roads and we began cutting them down. But there were too many roads leading into the woods for our work to be effective. Besides, the Germans used motorized field saws to cut through everything in their path. And they recruited neighboring farmers to clear the logs so tanks could penetrate the forest.

Early in the morning of Friday, September 18, we were summoned to a meeting by our political commanding officers. They read a radio message from the White Russian secretary of the Central Committee in Moscow, ordering the partisans to unite and to intensify their sabotage operations against the enemy. As we started to applaud the message, an airplane flying very low circled our camp. We were under close observation. At the same time we heard shooting just a few miles away. The officers ordered us to assume a defensive position. We camouflaged our food reserves, extra clothing and kitchen utensils. As the airplane came around again we dispersed to shelter. The rumor was that the Germans had launched a major attack against the partisans.

At two that afternoon we heard shooting from the direction of our patrol post, no more than a quarter of a mile from our camp. Seryosha, our political leader, ordered us to go deeper into the woods. As we lay flat beneath the foliage of the fallen trees, we saw partisans from a neighboring group running past, some of them wounded. It was the first group to be attacked: only 250 people to fight against thousands of Germans equipped with tanks and armed with machine guns and grenades. We later learned that 40,000 German troops had been ordered to fight the partisans in eastern Poland, White Russia and the Ukraine. With the retreat of one of our groups, the partisan opposition broke down and chaos prevailed. The central executive staff and its commander-in-chief left their camping place and disappeared deep in the woods.

Toward evening, our group of 350 gathered at a dry place, an island surrounded by mud and slime. It was getting dark and the shooting had quieted down. Seryosha told us we were to stay there for the night.

Yentl and her two children were overcome with fatigue. Rochele, the six-year-old, clung to her mother and cried that she was cold, wet and hungry. The infant, Matys, clung tightly to Yentl's dry breasts, sucking pus from her boils instead of milk.

Rochele had lost her shoes running through the woods and had cut her feet on the thorns. I took off my high-laced shoes and gave them to her to protect her soft feet as much as possible from the wild overgrown burdock and bramble. I was overcome with pain as I looked at my family, but I tried to comfort them: "Tomorrow it will quiet down; we'll go back to our camp and find food then." But all the while we smelled the smoke of our burning tents and huts. We slept little that night, praying that morning would never come, for we knew what awaited us.

At sunrise we heard the Germans shooting wildly. We gathered around Seryosha who was still calm, a trained soldier who had seen many battles. His instincts were quick and sensitive and he was able to endure stress, cold and hunger better than any of us. He not only knew how to use terrain for camouflage but he was an extraordinary night fighter. Calmly he listened, trying to pinpoint the German positions. The shooting seemed to get closer by the minute. Seryosha decided that we should divide into groups and that each group should move deeper into the woods, meanwhile keeping in contact with the others.

My sisters and I were in a group of about 100 people with Seryosha. We wandered through the woods the whole day. Everywhere we saw corpses of partisans. The boots of some of the dead had been removed and the pockets of their clothing turned inside out. Some lay on their backs with their eyes to the skies, as if they were saying: "See what you did to us!" I myself saw the bodies of friends with whom I had gone to school.

The weather was exceptionally hot and dry. Fear made us forget our hunger, but we could not overcome the parched feeling of our dry mouths. We were slowly dehydrating. The children cried with the last strength they possessed. Hearing their cries, the Germans stepped up their shooting and shouted, "Halt!" Seryosha, who had taken such devoted care of the babies and the small children, asked the mothers with infants to leave the rest of the group because they jeopardized the survival of all of us.

Yentl and her son joined five other women and their small children. They walked to a secluded area to stay overnight. Rochele did not want her mother to go and started to cry. I embraced her tightly and tried to assure her that next day we would all be together again.

The next morning, Sunday, the mothers came back to us carrying dead children. My sister was the only one whose baby was still alive. Rochele kissed and hugged her mother, but the reunion was not a joyful one. Yentl, her face the color of ash, lay bare the woes of the scene she had witnessed the night before.

"We couldn't keep our children quiet. They felt our fear and our restlessness. The woods have a language of their own, and every murmur of the leaves, every sound of a squirrel running in the trees made us panic. We were sure the enemy had found us. Suddenly Golda, who was sick and distraught over losing her husband, began wrapping her child with her shawl. With a terrible blank look on her face, she choked her baby to death. The rest of the mothers tried to stop her, but then something happened: they, too, became engulfed in some unexplainable madness—a kind of mass hysteria—and began to choke their babies to death.

"I stood there confused. Was I dreaming all this? Or was I witnessing a madness beyond my comprehension?" She paused in her recital, then added softly, "Look at them, Bryna. At what price we buy life."

It was heartbreaking to see the mothers rejoining their families. One man took his dead child from his wife and kissed it fervently, covering the body with a torrent of tears. One young mother knocked her head against a tree while her husband stood in a stupor, his dead child in his arms. We had to do something before the Germans, hearing our hysteria, discovered us.

A few men took the dead children from their mothers and placed them close together under a fallen tree, covering them with leaves and branches. We left them hurriedly because again we heard shots and wild shouts of "Halt, halt!" The woods were no longer big enough for us; the low-flying airplanes kept the Germans informed of our exact position.

Monday, the fourth day of the siege, Yentl could no

longer run. I took Matys from her arms; with my other hand I held my niece. As we ran, I kept calling my sisters to stay close and keep up with us.

We and the 15 people remaining in our group ran nearly 10 miles that day. Toward evening, when the shooting lessened, we stopped running and looked around to see who remained with us. Then I looked down to the baby in horror. He was black and blue, dead by suffocation. I must have held him too tightly. We cried and cursed the angry God who was not satisfied that the Germans, Lithuanians and White Russians were killing us but had to make us agents of death as well. I took off my slip and wrapped Matys in it.

With us was a pious man who kept praying no matter how great our suffering. He had a little hand shovel with him. I asked him to help us bury Matys, but he refused because it was not yet sundown and still Yom Kippur. I argued that it was more sinful to let a child's body be eaten by wolves than to help put him to his final rest. Finally he gave in, and under a huge old tree in the strange woods we buried Matys. Every year when I attend Yom Kippur services I pray only for forgiveness from my poor Matys. Before he had a chance to know life, he knew hunger, thirst, filth and a tragic death. All this, because he was born a Jew.

It was quieter the next day. We gathered berries, tried to dig for water with our bare hands and rested. Then we set out to search for others of our people. What we found were corpses. Some were tied to tree trunks, their tongues torn out, shoulders and arms wrenched from their sockets, hips bowed, knees turned inward, teeth clamped together, fingers bent in claws, faces contorted, eyeballs bulging and their private parts burned by fire. By these signs we knew that some of them had been captured alive. What we saw made us pray that if we had to die, it would be by bullet and not by slow torture. Many partisans kept loaded revolvers and were prepared to shoot themselves rather than fall into German hands.

In our wandering we came across a dead deer. Flies and vermin swarmed over the carcass and the smell was terrible. Still, we cut out its liver and roasted it over a little fire. Yentl refused to eat it; the sight made her nauseous. All of my pleadings did not help. Rochele's condition was almost as bad as her mother's. Her face was sunken, her body badly scratched by nettle weeds.

By Wednesday we were close to a highway that led to Moscow. About to cross, we saw some Germans trying to repair a tank. We lay flat on the ground and, miraculously, the Germans failed to notice us.

It seemed evident now, 10 days after the attack began, that the Germans were leaving. Our group decided to go back to our old camp, to look for other people as well as food and clothes. As we walked, I kept my little niece close to me, holding her by the hand most of the way. Yentl, too weak to take care of her, kept stumbling and falling. But by now the whole group was moving slowly and painfully so we managed to keep up. We listened for voices, hoping we could find other survivors and begin to reorganize in some way.

Wolcze Nory, when we finally spotted it, did not present the same vista we beheld when we first came to the woods. The farmers' houses had been burned to the ground. Bodies of men and animals lay in the ashes. Hoping to make it more difficult for the partisans to operate, the Germans had simply liquidated peasants who lived near the woods.

We walked on to the other side, a treeless hilly area where an abandoned Russian tank stood. It was some distance away, but my sister, Dalya, was far-sighted. "There are partisans behind the tank," she shouted. "They are motioning us to join them. Finally we have found friends!"

We were halfway there when Dalya appeared to freeze

in mid-stride. Her words now sent shivers through us: "We are trapped, we are trapped! The men wear black uniforms. It is the police."

Turning, we tried to make a hurried retreat into the woods, but low, thick bushes made it difficult to run. The police started to shoot and throw grenades. Soil, splinters and even bushes flew into the air. It seemed as if we were in the core of a volcanic eruption. We kept running but we could no longer see each other because of the smoke, dust and debris.

Within hours after the attack, I found Dalya and everyone else in our group except Yentl and Rochele. I prayed that they had merely wandered away or had met up with other survivors. I prayed in vain.

Six months later my worst fears were realized. Moshe Witkow from Byten told me that, alongside the roadway leading to the village of Kochanowo, he had seen seven corpses in a pile, some of them women and children. I asked him to take me to this place. Among the seven skeletons I recognized Yentl by the half-rotted fur collar on her coat. Only one of her legs still had flesh. My little niece I recognized by the high-laced shoes I had given her. It looked as if all seven people had been caught alive and burned on a bonfire.

Moshe helped me dig a grave. We buried all seven in the one pit. As he chanted the *El Molei Rachamin*, I thought of the irony of that psalm which praises our merciful God. I stood there numb and without tears, feeling only that life means nothing. Life suddenly snatched away becomes only a troubling dream, a persistent vapor. I raised my eyes to heaven; the burning sun was shining in undisturbed glory on an earth soaked with human blood. The ancient trees murmured tales of tragedies they had witnessed.

I should not, I told myself, have lost sight of them during the shooting. I should have held my niece's hand. When Yentl and Rochele needed me most I had not been there.

Had self-preservation overridden all my other instincts? Even though she was physically exhausted and distraught over the loss of her son, Yentl did retain presence of mind to hold on to her daughter. A passage from the Bible was fleeting through my mind: "Lovely and pleasant in their lives, and in their death they were not divided." I did not cry then at the grave of my sister and niece, but I have not stopped crying since.

I learned later that by walking toward the tank we had harmed not only ourselves but also a group of people hiding in the brush. There, close to potato fields, they had survived the 10 days of the German blockade. Had we not stepped into the trap, these people would have had a chance to survive the war.

8

In that attack on our Wolcze Nory woods, losses were depressingly heavy. From our Jewish group alone, only 170 survived out of 370. Small disorganized remnants of the group were scattered throughout the woods.

Now a new element of people began arriving. Some of the farmers managed to escape when the Germans began burning their villages. They came with their families, cows, horses and household items and they compounded our problems. Now it was difficult to tell who was partisan and who was spy. These farmers were hardly friends. Among them were anti-Semites who jeered us, calling us informers and cowards.

Late in October, 1942, 20 well-armed partisans from the Huta Michaliner woods visited our camp and asked us to cook potatoes for them. They were friendly at first and sometimes brought us meat and bread. This would soon change. Influenced by the farmers, they turned against us. They were led by a chief of staff who apparently believed that it was because of our group the Nazis attacked the woods and the villages around the woods. Anti-Semitic, the commander harassed us constantly. He allowed us to leave the woods only once a week to dig for the remaining potatoes.

As our difficulties continued, we decided to split our group of 170 into smaller sections. Our meager supply of potatoes and seeds was dwindling. There seemed to be but one thing for us to do—steal out of the forest and dig enough potatoes to last us for the winter. It was a dangerous undertaking since the fields were inspected constantly by the police and Germans.

As it turned out, the Germans were no more dangerous than the partisans themselves. On one of our trips from the fields a group of partisans ordered us to lie on the ground so they could search us. Then they robbed us of our better clothing and shoes. Detaining us for hours, they let us go with the warning that we would be shot if we were ever seen again in that vicinity. Another night, roving Wolcze Nory partisans not only robbed us but beat us with the butts of their rifles.

The Wolcze Nory partisans were now in complete domination of the forest. Desperate men, they badgered us constantly even though, by this time, we were barefoot and almost naked and had nothing left for them. Still, we didn't want to leave the forest; it was the safest place to hide. For temporary respite, we often changed our location in the woods, but the partisans always found us.

Seryosha, our political officer, was no longer with us. He and his Jewish sweetheart, Shaindel, were hiding somewhere in the woods. When the rulers of the forest eventually found Seryosha they demanded the gold and money he had collected from ghetto Jews who had escaped to the woods. He may have lost it or hidden it, but he had no treasure in his possession. So they "judged" him, found him guilty and ordered his execution. He was shot immediately. They did, however, spare his sweetheart's life. She was sent back to her people.

Another winter was approaching and we were soaked by cold, steady rains. In a way we waited for death. Yet, at the first sound of gunfire, we would spring to our feet. The children, the adults, the elderly, the ailing, the hungry—all were ready to run, to hide, to remain alive.

Early one morning, the partisan chief of staff gave us an ultimatum: leave the forest by the second of November or be shot. Other Jewish groups, faced with the same threat, chose to leave. Our group of 170 voted to stay. In the forest we had potatoes and were building earthen huts. Most felt that leaving would mean certain death.

Dalya and I, meanwhile, were part of a section of 15. At its head was Shmuel, the cartman, whose biggest asset was his extraordinary sense of direction. He knew every tree in the forest, the smallest dirt road and the surrounding villages as well. With him were his wife, Freidke, and his youngest daughter, age 10. An older daughter and son were in another forest. Shmuel, with a lack of sophistication but with a primitive sense of self-preservation, decided he would take no more persecution from the forest lords. Angrily, he shouted, "I escaped the bloody Germans and I will live in spite of the partisans, too, until I see them all 10 feet in the earth." He grabbed his wife and daughter and left. We who remained in his section rose and ran after him. Whether he wanted us or not, we were following him.

Leaving the rest of the 170 to fend for themselves in the forest, we wandered until we came to a thinly wooded area on dry terrain no more than five kilometers from Byten and not far from the railway station at Domanovo.

We rested for the night and then started to dig for shelter, scratching at the earth with our bare hands. We overlaid our small cave with logs and camouflaged it further with moss and autumn leaves. When we were through we could barely see it ourselves. We also started to dig a well by hand because we were afraid to go to the villages for water. Without a gun it would have been impossible to get anything from the peasants anyway, and villagers had been known to turn our people over to the Germans. The Germans would take them to the market places and torture them in front of crowds.

Every night around 10 o'clock, after the partisans returned to the forests from their operations, we would go to the fields and steal potatoes. First we had to steal into the villages for potato sacks. We would also take blankets off the backs of horses. After digging potatoes we carried them about seven kilometers back to our earthen hut, where we kept them in a camouflaged hole in the ground. Sometimes we brought carrots or raw cabbages, which were delicacies after the monotony of salt-free potatoes. We made cooking utensils from tin cans the German army had left behind. One of the cans, tied to a long rope, served as a pail to draw water from our well. Mostly we baked the potatoes because the water from the well was muddy.

We never left our earthen hut during the day because peasants were usually in the area, chopping trees for firewood. We cooked our meals at midnight when everybody was asleep so the smoke would go unnoticed. Our cave was so crowded we had to lie in two rows, the feet of one row at the heads of the other. If one person turned, the whole row had to turn. It was impossible to stretch.

One evening we were gathering driftwood when two men approached. They told us not to be alarmed; they were Jews from Slonim in search of other Jews. They were happy to find us but we were not happy to be found. We did not have an inch of space to spare, yet they insisted on staying. So we became a group of 17 in the tiny cave.

We were filthy and the white field lice gave us no rest. The weather grew severely cold, but we continued to dig frozen potatoes from the crusty earth. They were sweet and had a pinkish color when cooked.

By the end of November, heavy snow blanketed the woods and fields. The trips were now especially painful for me because I had no boots. I wrapped my feet in rags and tied them with string, but they would get wet from the snow and stiff from the cold. Walking on the plowed fields was like walking on sharp knives.

Afraid to leave footprints in the snow, we no longer walked on the roads but in the woods. We tried to return early enough from our trips for new snow to cover our footprints before sunrise. As the days wore on, our diet of frozen potatoes and the lack of salt became more and more a problem. Dora, a refugee from Lodz, became swollen and somewhat deranged. Boils festered on our infected bodies and the stench of pus was unbearable. We decided finally that five of us should take the risk of asking farmers for a little salt. I was one of the five. Knocking at the door of a farmer known to be sympathetic, we were given a basket of potatoes and black radishes but we were also told not to come back. The farmer explained he was under suspicion by the Germans. He added that farmers near the woods whose buildings had been burned by the Germans usually dug cellars. Perhaps unburnt food might be hidden there. We thanked the good peasant and left.

We were only a few feet from the door when we heard "Halt!" All five of us started to run in different directions but I lagged behind because the uneven chunks of earth cut into my feet, and a cough I developed in the cave made me wheeze with every breath. Grabbed by the collar, I was led toward two armed men. Three armed men were behind me.

"Tell us where the partisan camps are located," one of them asked, his rifle leveled at me. "We will let you free if you will lead us to them. How many of them are there in the woods?"

I answered that I knew nothing about partisans. A man behind me jabbed me with the butt of his rifle and shouted, "You are a liar. You live in the woods and never see a partisan?"

"That's correct."

"You swine! What sabotage work are the partisans about to execute against the German Wehrmacht and us, the police?"

"I told you, I don't know. I'm just a Jewish girl hiding in the woods."

"We should take you to your town's market place and hang you there, to show people what we do to partisans when we catch them."

I had heard of such incidents and pleaded with them to spare me the torture. "Be kind and kill me right here," I asked. "You are human; you must have some conscience, or even children my own age. Think what they would feel in my place. I am only asking you the favor of killing me here on the spot."

"Stay here," they commanded and went behind the barn for a brief meeting.

I shivered. The night was bright but bitter cold. The full moon shone over the fields. A fleeting thought passed through my mind: only the moon will witness the final moments of my life. "My dear family," I whispered, "let my sinful soul join you. I pray that Dalya survives the war."

For that brief moment I was free from fear. Then I heard one of the men say, "You are free; go to your people."

All I could think of was that it must be a trick. They hoped I would lead them to my people so they could kill them. I hesitated and then started moving into the woods, not on the road but among the trees. Every few minutes I stopped to listen, but I heard no one follow me.

Now I grew nervous because I thought I was lost. Then I heard someone call my name. It was Dodl. He had seen me in custody and was afraid to return to the shelter in case the police made me reveal our hiding place. He had let me pass him and then fell in behind me.

When I told him what had happened, we began to surmise that the men hadn't really been local police, but partisans testing us. We decided it was safe to go back to our hut. Not until morning, when the other three members of our party returned separately, did we tell our people about the the incident. They hugged and kissed me and told me how brave I was and how much they respected me.

Six months later, after we again joined the partisans, we learned that our theory about the "local police" had been correct. We met the partisans who caught me. They said they didn't shoot me because they admired my courage. No matter how they tried to scare me, I didn't give the partisans away. My asking to be killed and my physical condition made them take pity on me. Not until much later, when I learned that the partisans had killed many of the Jews they had caught and tested, did I realize how lucky I was.

9

For a few nights following my capture, we did not leave our shelter at all. Our shattered nerves needed to be calmed. When we did venture out we looked for burned-out farm houses. We walked eight miles before we came to one. We found salt mixed with sand, straw and soot and collected a sackful. Then one woman picked up what she thought was a cow's head, thinking it could be used to make soup. After closer inspection she realized she was holding a human skull. In the ashes, she also discovered the bodies of children clustered in an area under the big oven where farmers kept their chickens during winter. Hiding in the chicken coop, the children must have been burned alive when the house was set afire.

In the yard between the house and barn we found a cellar full of potatoes. Hastily we filled our sacks and brought them back to our hut. Once there, we put them away for the days when we wouldn't be able to venture forth. This cellar of potatoes was to save our lives.

Dodl had a friend in the village of Zarechye, just half a mile from Byten. He was sure he could get bread and flour from the peasant, and maybe even salt. I volunteered to go with him. Approaching the village through fields and gardens, we had a little trouble finding the house in the dark. Dogs in the village started barking as we scouted around. When we finally found the house, the frightened farmer told us we were risking not only our lives but his, since the barking dogs had undoubtedly aroused the police. He did, however, give Dodl a loaf of bread and seven pounds of flour, his teeth chattering with fear.

We had left Zarechye and were about half a mile away when we heard shooting and the sound of motorcycles. We ran as fast as we could without looking back.

The fields had clusters of snow-covered bushes that hid us from the police and we made it back to our camp alive. For the next few days we feasted. We cooked potato soup with dumplings made out of the rye flour and we all began to feel a little better. Dodl, however, would not share his loaf of bread with us. Every night he cut a slice and ate it while we were asleep.

Night after night we made the seven or eight-mile trek to the cellar at the burned-out farmhouse. Half naked and without shoes, I carried 30 to 40 kilograms of potatoes on my back. We could not stop to rest for fear of being caught by Germans or partisans. I had a hard time keeping up. Whenever I stumbled or fell, someone came along to help and adjusted the sack of potatoes on my shoulders.

My cough bothered me more and more; I could no longer straighten up. I overheard friends talking among themselves, saying that I was dying with tuberculosis. They marveled at the way I kept going. I never stayed behind; I went wherever my people went. Those who remained in the shelter were sick or frail. They cooked and cleaned and, with the rest of us gone, they could stretch their legs, an impossible feat when all 17 of us were inside.

Dalya was among those who remained in the cave and didn't take part in the nocturnal expeditions. She couldn't endure the long trips or the heavy loads. Deep in my heart I was glad. It was bad enough that one of us was exposed to the danger of being caught and killed.

Early in the morning of January 20, 1943, I had crawled

from the hut to take care of my bodily eliminations when suddenly I heard German voices shouting, "Halt!" I threw myself on the ground, sure that the Germans had discovered our hut. We had made our usual trip for potatoes the previous night; now I was afraid our footprints had been detected. I lay stretched out in the snow for an hour before the voices faded. By then I realized the soldiers were yelling "Halt" to confuse anyone who might be hiding, to trick us into believing we had been spotted.

Back in the hut, I found that the others had heard the Germans, too. But luck had been with us. Fresh snow had covered our tracks and the Germans, not really expecting that anybody would be hiding so close to Byten, didn't search too thoroughly.

Now we decided to stay under cover and not go out for any reason. The trips for food were discontinued until the snow melted so that we would not leave a trail. By this time most of the available potatoes had been transferred to the cave, enough to sustain us for a month or more. From then on, each of us received a daily allotment of five potatoes, which we baked at night. The days were the quietest we experienced in our two years in the woods. But there were nervous moments ahead.

On the night of March 18, we went foraging again, leaving a few women behind. We had difficulty finding a farm in the dark and day was beginning to break when we finally filled our sacks. A dense fog soon settled over the countryside. Disoriented, we began to walk in the direction of the village of Kochanowa. By the time we discovered our error and returned to the cave, the women were in tears. Because of the lateness of the hour they were sure we had been caught and killed.

We had barely sat down to rest when a loud voice near the lid of our cave sent shivers down our spines. "It is not very smart to leave fresh footprints," the gruff voice said. We panicked, certain the police had discovered us. When a few minutes passed and nobody entered the cave, we thought we were being blockaded. I said, "I'll go out and test them. If they let me out, they must be partisans." One of the women answered, "You are always daring, but we have nothing to lose. A grenade will finish us off." When I crawled out from our hovel, two armed men stood there staring at me. Behind them was a horse and a cart full of sacks. Struggling to keep my voice calm, I asked, "What brings you here?"

"Your footprints, silly. Don't you know better? When we saw your trail in an area where no partisans camp, we decided to investigate."

Relieved, I invited the partisans in to meet us. After so long in seclusion, we were hungry for company. Inspecting our shelter, the two visitors could not understand how we survived. "How do you fit in here, like sardines in a can?", one of them asked. "How do you get your food?" Everybody started to talk at once.

Friedke, Shmuel and Berl unbuttoned their ragged clothes and exposed their running sores clogged with mud, lice, blood and pus. "We have these boils because we have had no salt for half a year. We live on potatoes we steal at night. That is the reason for the footprints."

"But why do you live like this?" one partisan asked.

"What could we do?" I replied. "You surely must know that the partisans ordered us to leave the woods last October under the threat of death! What option had we? We protested, but the partisans ordered us to go back to our people in our towns, knowing that there were no more Jews left. We decided to hide here, close to Byten, out of the way of the partisans and out of the way of the Germans."

"You will be happy to know that your Jewish group of partisans is still in Wolcze Nory. They refused to leave the woods. Besides, there is an order from the partisan chief of staff that any group that is discovered must join the partisans; no one is allowed in the woods without supervision or authority of the staff. For your own safety, you should join your Jewish group."

The news that other Jews survived filled us with elation. This was contrary to what we read in a German newspaper we found near a farm. On New Year's Day of 1943, Hitler had boasted that no more Jews were left in Europe. We were lonely, too, for human contact. Besides we knew we could not survive without an organized partisan outfit. When our two visitors offered us little gifts of salt and flour, we were delighted we had been discovered after all.

10

Finding the Jewish group required a whole day of walking for Shmuel, Dodl and me. They looked pitiful, neither as healthy nor rested as we. Fewer than 70 people remained of the 170 who were alive in October of 1942. They poured out an account of their lives and times.

This is their story:

When you left our group, sometime in November, we decided to stay in the woods. Near the end of the month, an ex-lieutenant in the Red army by the name of Bobkov and two other men arrived in a sled harnessed to a white horse. They sat down to a campfire and asked us to assemble.

Bobkov started his speech by referring to our potential usefulness to the partisan movement, but added, "Don't just sit in the woods! Go out and fight the enemy."

We all spoke up at once. "Who is to blame for our inactivity, if not you—the partisans? You're making a ghetto for us Jews here in the woods! You chase us out under the threat of death or you confine us to our camp."

"You don't deserve any better," Bobkov retorted. "You were German spies before the

German attack on the woods. Because of you, many good partisans lost their lives."

We vehemently objected to his lies. We told him he talked like the Germans. One of the others, a young man from Russia, tried to calm us, "I have heard a lot of these charges against you and I am sure many of the things I have heard are not true. Your brothers in Russia are fighting and working hard. Looking at you I see you are a fine group of people, capable of applying your skills to our underground work. Please try to organize yourselves so you will be ready to begin."

Bobkov gave us four rifles and bullets and ordered us to elect a commander. He gave us permission to go to the village for food. He also gave us assignments: by January 10, 1943, we were to cut all telephone lines between the cities of Slonim and Ryzenoj; by January 25, we were to derail a train carrying German soldiers to the front. He promised to supply us with dynamite and tools. He still forbade us to wander through the woods and told us to move our camp to the Rafalovka Woods.

Again, we objected. The Rafalovka Woods offered little protection, we argued; the police would have little difficulty finding us. We suspected they wanted us killed. Bobkov replied, "An order is an order," and the three Russians left.

We were heartsick. It had taken us a month to build our huts for the winter and now, in the bitter cold and the ground frozen, we had to start all over again. We had no alternative but to leave our Wolcze

Nory camp and trudge to a more vulnerable location. Exhausted when we finally reached the pine forest, we slept through the night at a bonfire.

Next morning we split into two groups of 75 each, one to provide food and the other to build shelters. Small teams of 15 worked day and night on the shelters. Picks had to be used to split the stone-hard ground. There was no water to drink; we had to melt snow or chop through the marshy ground two miles away. We lived mostly on baked potatoes and drank muddy water.

But we fulfilled Bobkov's order. Seventeen boys from our group cut down 80 telephone poles, some no farther than three kilometers from Slonim. Later we read in the local German newspaper that "hundreds" of partisans had destroyed kilometers of telephone communications and that it took German technicians three days to fix them. Then, with an artillery shell weighing 60 kilograms, we began to work on derailing a German train.

December 24 was especially cold. At 11 p.m., the sound of German artillery sent us scurrying to extinguish fires and running to hiding places. After the shooting stopped, we listened to the festive singing of German soldiers from one direction, and White Russian conversations from another. Intermixed with the sounds of Christmas mirth were sounds of anguish from the village of Okinowo.

Shooting recommenced toward morning and grew closer. By noon, the Germans were all around us. We could hear them saying, "Where did the leprous devils hide?" They knew we were near because the ashes from our fires were still warm. They began throwing hand grenades into the places that were overgrown with brush. One grenade fell into the shelter where Boris, our assistant commander, and his small group were hiding. Boris picked up the grenade and threw it out as it exploded. Everyone in the group was injured, but none uttered a cry, so as not to alert the enemy.

Not until night fell were we able to crawl out of our caves, straighten our cramped limbs and breathe the fresh, delicious air of the woods. We found our camp in ashes and nine people dead.

Our patrol to the village of Okinowo found most of the village destroyed and the farmers killed. It was their lamentations we had heard on Christmas night. Their livestock was now free and unguarded, so our patrol brought back some of the animals, along with carts loaded with food. The partisans, learning our group survived the attack, were astonished. Cruelly, they joked: "Even bullets don't kill you."

Next day, intelligence reports reached the chief of staff that the Germans would return to Okinowo and strip the village. The partisans and some of our young men hid in the village and waited. A bitter fight ensued, lasting half a day and leaving many dead and wounded on both sides.

On January 15, by order of the chief of staff, our group burned several houses in the

village of Suchinka, homes of peasants who
were German informers. Two days later, our
patrol captured three carriages carrying
peasants, three of whom we recognized as
the biggest criminals in Byten. They had robbed, killed and terrorized the Jews in the
ghetto. When we took them to the chief of
staff, they confessed to being spies for the
Germans. They were shot immediately and
we were praised for our efficiency.

Five days later, very early in the morning,
a shot was fired and one of our guards fell.
Another ran to the camp and warned us of an
attack. Hellish gunfire broke out before we
could flee from our campfire. In confusion,
our people began running in the direction of
Wolcze Nory woods. Soon we heard the
sound of galloping horses; the partisans were
coming to our rescue. After half an hour of
intensive shooting, the invaders were routed
and we returned to our camp.

Our meager possessions were strewn over
the ground. Shivering with cold and fear we
started to look for our children. We didn't
have to look far. We found a row of
youngsters on the ground with shattered
heads and torn limbs. (Moshe breaks into the
conversation.) "In the shrubbery we found
our daughter, shot dead in the breast and not
far from her brother. We picked him up, and
blood gurgled from his head. A bullet was
stuck just above his eye. We took him to the
hut, boiled water and tried to feed him, but
he couldn't open his mouth. Half of his body
was paralyzed and frozen. With each day he
got worse, pus running over his face, frozen

flesh falling off his body. My wife, Esther,
tended him and the other wounded—25 in
all—day and night, until she died of fatigue
and the pain of losing her children."

Later we learned from two Jewish brothers
from Kosov, who fought heroically with the
Russian partisans, that no Germans took part
in the attack on our camp. Our attackers
were 80 policemen from Byten.

When we notified our chief of staff that we
had lost 55 people, his answer was, "Now
that you have lost much of your garbage, you
are a small and healthy group. It will be
easier for you to survive the war."

March 12, 1943, we were allowed to
return to Wolcze Nory—where six months
ago we had been a group of 370 people. Now
we are less than a hundred, but we have con-
soled ourselves with the coming of spring.

Shmuel, Dodl and I slept that night at Wolcze Nory and
returned to our people the next morning. The 17 of us who
were cave dwellers voted to delay our return to Wolcze
Nory. We concluded that, as long as our potatoes lasted, we
were much safer where we were. Away from the partisans,
our place was not suspected by the police or the Germans.

Not until April 5 did we rejoin our brethren in Wolcze
Nory. Then we learned how wise we were to wait: an attack on the camp on March 20 had taken 21 lives.

We now found a situation in the Jewish camp that had
not existed before. Men who had lost their wives and
women who had lost husbands developed intimate ties. The
men became protectors of the women they chose and tried
to supply them with food and clothing. Young men with no
families had no desire to risk their lives for women and
children. They asked the chief of staff to incorporate them
into the partisan brigade.

The Jewish boys quickly proved themselves in combat. In the village of Koroszcze, they waited side-by-side with partisans to intercept Germans who planned to take young peasants from the area to labor camps. Ambushing four truckloads of Germans, they were able to kill the soldiers and confiscate their weapons. One by one, the stronger men left our group permanently to join the fighters. Our situation became more precarious until the Jewish fighters moved back to our woods and camped about half a kilometer from our family unit.

On the other side of the Szczara river, 34 kilometers from the Wolcze Nory woods, lived a group of 45 Jews who managed to survive the winter of 1942-43 without being discovered by either Germans or partisans. Now the partisans chanced upon them and ordered them to join our group. We were happy to have the newcomers because they were strong and healthy. They were less pleased because they had suffered less and had not been attacked. But we merged into a single group and began collecting guns of our own. Our mission now was to supply food for the chief of staff and stand guard over the partisan camps.

The final raid on our camp came in July. Very early in the morning we were awakened in our huts by heavy sniper fire. The partisans began leaving their camp and told us to leave ours. The woods were being attacked from two directions by Byten police and police from Iwacewicze and Kosov. One unit of partisans took up defensive positions three kilometers from our camp, while the rest of us retreated deep into the woods. The police burned our camp but could take no lives. It was totally different from the raid on March 20 which led to 21 Jewish corpses. The difference was this: on March 20, the partisans retreated without giving warning and returned when the attackers were gone.

11

Once again my sister and I were members of a family group. I was 18, independent by nature and the only girl who took the same jobs as the men. I stood guard nearly every day and also accompanied groups hunting food. A few men asked me to become their sweetheart, but romance was strange to me. I didn't look for love and didn't want anybody risking his life for me.

I was a pretty girl in spite of what I had gone through. My hair was blond and curly, my face full of freckles and I had a good figure. A high-ranking member of the partisan staff offered our people six guns if they would persuade me to join his camp. To have the protection of partisan might and power was an offer of life, but I couldn't bring myself to do it. As an indication of the decency prevailing in the woods, none of my group pressured me even though a bribe of six guns was difficult to pass up.

As if we didn't have trouble enough in the summer of 1943, an epidemic of typhus broke out. There was but one doctor, a Jew, to take care of the 3,000 partisans in the woods. Often delirious, the sick ran high fevers for 10 days. After the crisis passed, it took two weeks before they could walk without help. Meanwhile their hair had fallen out; women as well as men remained bald for as long as a year. Miraculously there were no deaths from typhus, except for

a visiting Russian colonel. The partisans had become
hardened by life in the woods, sleeping in mud in summer
and in snow in winter. Only the colonel, who was soft by
comparison, could not withstand the typhus.

From the same colonel came our first hope that we might
live to see Germany defeated. He told us that in a spec-
tacular campaign in July and August, the Americans,
British and Canadians conquered the island of Sicily. The
fascist regime of Mussolini had fallen.

One evening that summer I joined four others in a visit to
Kochanowo for food. The head of our group was Lejzer
Wesnick, a young man of 19, handsome, tall, and with an
extraordinary sense of direction. He knew every footpath,
every corner, every tree in the woods. He was the jewel of
our group, a most devoted and reliable member. With him
in the woods were his mother, his younger sister and his
sweetheart. They were among our 17 people, the cave
dwellers, who for half a year lived in fear of the partisans as
well as the Germans. Quite often, the men assigned to provide food for the group snooped around in a farmer's
cellar and helped themselves to a piece of butter or a pot of
sour milk which they would bring back to their sweethearts
as a special treat, concealing it from the communal kitchen. Lejzer was an exception. He never sneaked
anything to his family.

On this particular evening in the village, we knocked on
a farmer's door and demanded two sacks of potatoes and a
loaf of bread. From another farmer, Lejzer obtained a cow,
which he tied to our wagon. Starting to leave the village,
we were suddenly caught in a crossfire; rockets lit the
village as though it were daylight. As bullets whistled
around us, we left the horse and wagon and ran through
gardens and meadows in the direction of the woods. This
time I looked around as I ran to make sure I wouldn't be
separated from the others. In that instant I saw Lejzer
tumble over, blood oozing from his mouth. With the

Samochova, the local police, close behind, none of us could stop to help him. Confused, we kept running, not knowing where we were running. Half an hour later, only Dodl and I were together. We had lost sight of our two friends. The shooting had stopped, danger had passed so we sat down to rest. We sat for a long time, waiting to see if anyone else had escaped and dreading to face Lejzer's mother and sweetheart. Finally, when we did return, our faces mirrored the sadness in our hearts. The camp waited for us in a state of agitation. An outburst of cries echoed through the woods when we revealed that Lejzer had been struck by a bullet and that we knew nothing of our two other companions. The loss of Lejzer was too much to bear. Everybody loved him. He was our main breadwinner, our treasure, the core of our group.

Three days went by without news of the other two. To our great surprise, they arrived on the fourth day, safe but hungry and wet. In the confusion of the shooting they had run a couple of miles before hiding, flat on their stomachs, in heavy grass near a railway station. Then they saw Germans guarding the tracks. They remained pinned there for three days, afraid to move. In the rain and darkness of the third night they made their escape by crawling out of the area on their hands and knees.

Time now seemed to pass more slowly. We began to breathe freer, especially in the evenings. We could read between the lines of German newspapers that not everything was going well with the German armies. Naturally the Germans did not write about their defeats but they didn't have to.

Frequently, Russian paratroopers descended into the woods, and underground activities perked up under their guidance. An airfield was built. Sometimes, when Russian planes were expected, we made fires to show them where to drop ammunition. The partisans, sensing their mother country was close to victory, became fretful about their reputation for hostility toward us. Communism preaches humanitarianism, equality and brotherly love. But the partisans' hatred for Jews was so deeply rooted that they still could merely tolerate us.

During this time we were heartened to hear that an American-British-Russian conference was held in Moscow from October 19 to October 30, 1943, and that now the three nations were jointly planning their military campaigns.

On our front, partisan activities were increasingly effective. Hardly a night passed in which partisans did not derail trains, destroy miles of track, disrupt telephone service and harass the German garrisons. The railroad sabotage was especially fruitful because the Germans had to keep the trains moving to bring back frostbitten soldiers from the Russian front and to supply the front with new troops and food.

In March, 1944, the Germans assailed our woods again and sent us retreating to a forest four miles away. As I ran through mud and snow, I felt my legs collapsing under me. My head was a flaming furnace. To keep up with the others, I threw away my patched coat. We were on the run most of the day, my legs unsteady every inch of the way. At dusk, when the shooting abated, we lay down to rest. We were afraid to make a fire, and to keep warm we lay in a row snuggled against one another. Burning and at the same time shaking with chills, I moved close to a man who wore a long sheepskin coat. Unbuttoning his coat, he put part of it over me to give me some protection from the cold. Dalya covered me on the other side.

The next morning my body was livid with red spots. It was typhus. Six months after the epidemic had passed—six months after my sister and everybody else had been struck —I had to get sick. And the only doctor was in another forest with the partisans. I couldn't even get an aspirin.

For 14 days I faced death. My fever remained high but I

was not unconscious of what went on around me. My sister, who kept vigil over me, told me later that I did talk and sing in my sleep. Even on the 14th day, when the crisis passed and my temperature returned to normal, I was unable to get up. Like the other typhus victims, I had to take walking lessons. Fortunately, the woods were peaceful during my convalescence. In two weeks I could walk without my sister's help, but now my wavy, blond hair started to fall out by the handful. Soon I was completely bald. I was nothing but skin and bones; I had lost even my freckles. One of our people brought me a babushka, which I didn't remove from my head for a very long time. A year later when my new hair grew in, it was kinky, like sheep's wool.

Within two months there was another scare. A rumor circulated that a special German battalion had been ordered from the front, and that they were bringing cadres of dogs trained to search and kill, leaving no chance for survival. Fear mounted in us at the thought of German dogs trapping us in our hiding places. We prayed that, if our time came, death would be delivered by bullets penetrating us while we were running. But we went on constructing better caves and hideouts.

Daily the mood of local German authorities and police grew more somber and depressed. Strong walls were built around their station posts; barricades of sandbags went up. No German would leave his post by himself; for their safety they moved about only in groups. At the same time, the partisans became bolder.

In the early days of July, 1944, multitudes of Russian planes darkened the skies. We knew then that the harassed Germans no longer had time to mount an attack on the partisans. At long last, we had the upper hand.

Monday night, July 9, the sounds of artillery grew near. Red army patrols entered the woods the next morning. They ordered the partisans to congregate in one place, to prevent their being fired upon by mistake. The woods were full of local police and civilians who had collaborated with the Germans. They were fleeing now from Russian tanks, heavy artillery and trucks. And, step by step, the Russian armies moved after the retreating Germans.

Part Five: Toward freedom

12

A Russian colonel brought us the word. He told us—the women, the children and the older men—that we could return home. The young men were recruited into the Red army.

Of the 370 Jews who had escaped from the Byten ghetto, only 23 now lived. At that, we had fared better than many big Jewish communities in Poland where not a single man, woman or child survived.

For the last time, we walked through the woods with its blood-soaked roads and footpaths. As we walked, we saw the corpses of White Russian policemen who had collaborated with the Germans. Tied to trees, their tongues torn out and their genitals burned by fires, they had been treated by partisans the same way the Germans had treated captured partisans.

Passing through villages, we stopped to ask for bread. We were hungry, barefoot and had only rags for clothes. Our White Russian neighbors refused to help us. They told us they had enough of the partisans who had robbed them. They were no longer afraid, they said. The truth was, they did not want us to come into their houses and see the furniture and clothing they had taken from the Jews in the ghettos.

When Dalya and I arrived back in Byten, we decided

against going back to our own house because it stood by the mill, detached from the city. We were afraid of our neighbors and expected the worst from the peasants. We went instead to Yentl's house in the city proper.

An old peasant woman whom we knew now lived in the house with her two sons. We gave her two weeks' notice and allowed her to dig up half the potatoes planted in the garden. We were still hungry. For all we knew, the potatoes would be our only sustenance. The potato peelings we gave to a woman who did our laundry before the war. In exchange she gave us some milk.

One day I braced myself and went up to our grain mill, now the property of the Red army. Hearing my story, one of the officers gave me ten pounds of flour. Once again we were able to break the monotony, for a while, of our diet of saltless potatoes.

We soon learned that the NKVD had gathered furniture and other possessions from places that housed local German authorities and the Samochova, the White Russian police who served them. In the storage place, we spotted our wardrobe locker and bedroom set and hauled them home. With the permission of the NKVD, we also took a couple of pillows, an old blanket, a pot and a few dishes. Our clothing situation did not improve. We still wore the ragged dresses from the woods and we were still barefoot.

On July 25, the memorial day of the liquidation of our ghetto two years earlier, we, the 23 survivors, visited the grave. Sheep grazed near the spot and a small shepherd boy stood by. The place was overgrown with weeds, and pigs roamed among the sheep. Still, the gravesite evoked the most poignant memories of life with our families and dear ones, of people who were no more. Our souls cried, and it seemed to us that everything around cried with us—the fields, the valleys, the hills, even the birds in the trees. The sound of crying had become part of us, and even part of nature. We prostrated ourselves on the ground and mixed our tears with the soil, once saturated with Jewish blood.

Then we tidied up the grave, which was 48 meters long and 6 meters wide. We dug a ditch around it so animals would not graze there. Finally we chanted *"Al mole rachamin"* ("O merciful God") and I stood there speaking in a loud voice to my dead mother, my father and to my sister, Henia, to whom Dalya and I owe our lives. I cried again for my little brother, Chaim. With my hot and salty tears falling to the grave, I asked forgiveness for my sins against them and for the heavy burden of guilt I carry for not taking proper care of my sister, Yentl, and her two children in the woods.

A year later, before leaving Byten for good, we put a fence around the grave and marked it with stones.

Meanwhile, the attitude of the Soviet government toward us was helpful. They gave us jobs in offices and shops. Because I had knowledge in this area, they made me head bookkeeper in the office of commerce and industry in our county. I received 550 rubles a month, for which I couldn't buy so much as a loaf of bread. It was still wartime and money was worthless. Farmers preferred to barter their goods, rather than sell. The government stores were nearly empty. In spite of my relatively high position, I still did not have a decent pair of shoes. In Yentl's house, I found an old pair that had belonged to my brother-in-law and in these big shoes I went to work. Dalya, not knowing any trade, remained unemployed.

I was the only non-Party member who could shop in the government stores. From time to time I bought a little salt, some bread, a little cereal and, once, even a couple of pieces of chocolate. I was also admitted to the only restaurant in town, which catered to Communist Party people, the NKVD and the police. But very seldom did I take advantage of this privilege. I was never at ease there;

besides, they served only watery potato soup with an occasional piece of meat in it.

In spite of the hard life and the scarcity of food, we had no complaints against the Russians. They fared no better than we. The Russian government taxed the farmers, who had to deliver a prescribed amount of potatoes, grain and cattle to supply the Russian armies. These taxations went through the office where I worked.

Once, my director, who was Russian and a Party member but who knew my money could buy little food, advised me to go to the warehouse and steal a few sacks of potatoes while the soldiers loaded their trucks. I was never to tell anybody about it, he warned. He and I would surely go to jail if word got out.

One day a Red army lieutenant came to our office with an order for potatoes too large for us to fill. His battalion was passing through our region and his soldiers were not only poorly clothed but hungry. When we told him that our sandy soil simply could not yield food enough for all the passing troops, the lieutenant became furious and pounded my desk with his fists. He screamed that I and the director sat behind desks with folded hands and refused to help his soldiers, even with potatoes. Our hearts bled for him, but we could do little. Much of the Russian army was hungry.

My assistant bookkeeper, a young lady from a small town near Moscow, told us of the starvation there. People ate grass roots, picked up potato peelings from German kitchens and got scraps of food from German soldiers in exchange for doing their laundry. She said her parents were swollen from hunger. In 1941, when the Russian armies retreated, they burned villages and fields to keep food from the conquerors. But their own people suffered as a consequence.

Conditioned in the woods, I and other Jews in Byten could bear the hardships of the time. But as night came on and I left my office for home, a sense of aloneness would come over me. As I walked, the people who had inhabited the streets just two years earlier came to mind. In moments of forgetfulness, I would feel the urge to drop in on them for a chat. But now, White Russians from adjacent villages occupied the Jewish homes.

For two reasons we did not mix with the local population. First, the majority of them had collaborated with the Germans. If it had not been for them, many more Jews would have had a chance to survive. Had they sympathized with us, they could have helped us hide in the fields or on their farms. Instead, the local police attacked us in the woods and helped the Germans in their solution of the Jewish problem—total liquidation. The second reason we did not mix was that we did not have common ground for communication. Most of them were illiterate, crude in their customs and habits. None of them subscribed to a newspaper. They lived in ignorance. Their only pleasure was to come to the market place and get drunk after disposing of their produce. Most of their work went for whiskey.

The Jews in our group were hard working. According to Polish law, we could not be farmers. We were forbidden to own land. Most Jews were shopkeepers and tradespeople, and competition among them was intense. Even as a child, I disliked the life of the storekeeper and his way of conducting business. Labor in Poland was very cheap. The shoemakers, carpenters and tailors worked for pennies. But the Jews were frugal and knew how to manage their money. Their prime concern was to educate their children. Every Jewish mother dreamed that her son would be a rabbi or a doctor. Poor or rich, every Jewish house subscribed to at least one daily publication, and the majority had Polish and Jewish daily papers delivered to their homes as well as magazines of all kinds.

Young Jews dreamed of leaving the small towns and traveling all over the world. They were romantic and restless. They were familiar with world literature and faraway places lured them like a magical force. They were also ardent students of Jewish law.

Being of a Semitic race, we differed also from the Gentile population in our physique and appearance. We were not as robust as the majority of the Gentiles. Jewish boys were often pale and slight, spending most of the time over their books or in the *Yeshiva*, the school for rabbis, and they had no inclination for athletics. They didn't fight and they didn't drink. Their family ties were closely knit.

With this traditional upbringing, with such a difference in our outlook on life, we few survivors could not feel comfortable with the local population. We felt more lonesome with each passing day. We were hungry for a Jewish face, a Jewish book, a Jewish environment, a Jewish life. With nostalgia we recalled our lives with our families. We looked to the future with apprehension. My sister and I were of marriageable age, but with our upbringing and heritage we could never marry non-Jews.

We dreamed of joining our brother, Nathan, and other relatives in the United States, but we didn't see how our dreams could be realized. Free movement in Poland was not allowed. People were tied to their jobs and couldn't change them.

Our city hall received many letters of inquiry from American people who had relatives in Byten, but no inquiry had been made about our family. I had paid 35 rubles to the Anti-Fascist Movement in Moscow to help me find my relatives in the States, but a year passed and I heard nothing.

One day, early in the summer of 1945, our friend, Dodl, who was with us in the woods and later recruited into the Red army, returned home. He had aged terribly, and an armless sleeve was tucked under his belt.

Like the other partisans who were Polish citizens before the war, he had been assigned by the army to the Polish unit. When the Red army pushed close to Warsaw, the

Polish unit requested that it alone liberate Poland's capital city. The request was granted even though Russian leaders knew full well that the Polish forces were not strong enough to take the heavily fortified city.

Not until the Polish unit was destroyed in its vain effort did the Red army storm and take Warsaw. In the battle, Dodl saw all his friends killed. Two years of torture and deprivation in the woods were not enough; they had yet to die on the battlefield. Dodl was the only one of our young Jewish partisans to survive. He lay wounded and unconscious until the Reds took Warsaw and sent their casualties back to hospitals. There, they amputated his arm. No longer of use to the army, he was discharged and he returned to Byten.

About this time, people who had been Polish citizens in 1939 and who were now living in Russian territory were given the opportunity to move into Poland. I tried to persuade my friends to take advantage of the situation. I told them we would bitterly regret it later if we let this opportunity slip. I insisted that we give up our Russian citizenship and ask to be released from our jobs, but everybody refused. They were afraid of the consequences.

Then news reached us that surviving Jews from Baranowicze, Slonim, Iwacewicze and Kosov had already signed up to leave. At that, all my friends changed their minds. We notified the office of resettlement of our decision to reclaim our Polish citizenship, explaining that we wanted to find some kind of Jewish social life in a bigger community and, when the war was over, possibly to join our relatives abroad. The officials told us they had no reason to hold us back.

On August 10, 1945, we visited the mass grave for the last time. Then we went home, picked up our small bundles of food and possessions and walked to the railroad station at Domanovo to wait for a train to take us to Poland.

By the sheerest coincidence, that very day Dalya and I

received a letter from the Red Cross giving the addresses of our relatives in the United States. Hope kindled again at the possibility that we might join our relatives in a new world and a new home.

13

On a hot August afternoon, we boarded the freight train that was to take us to Poland. Each of us picked a corner where we lodged our bundles, which would serve as seats. Our aim was to reach Warsaw. We were sure that in the city that had the largest Jewish population before the war we would find some kind of organized Jewish life.

The trip took two weeks. At every station we got off to stretch our aching limbs. We also gathered firewood to cook a hot meal—usually potatoes or barley soup. There was continuous movement of trains going back to Russia, most of them loaded with machinery and equipment; whole factories were being transported. The Russians were making sure that Germany was stripped of her industrial potential, that her recovery would be delayed. Besides, Russia could make good use of every screw, pipe and tire it transported. Russia was poor, beset by shortages of virtually everything. Returning Russian soldiers carried with them sacks of German marks and Polish zlotys. At every stop, they got off to buy merchandise from the Poles, who peddled their wares at trackside. The soldiers turned over sacks of zlotys for a watch or a pair of boots and bought eggs by the dozens.

We carried with us Russian rubles, which were worthless

back in Byten. We could buy nothing with them there, not even on the black market. Now we exchanged our rubles with the Russian soldiers for Polish zlotys and made very good deals.

Free commerce was not forbidden in Poland, but prices on the free market were sky-high. Twenty zlotys, which earlier would have supported a family of four for a week, now bought only a loaf of bread. But we were glad to be able to get it, no matter what the price.

Warsaw, when we finally reached it, shocked us. The city lay in ruins and ashes. The Warsaw Poles were trying to rebuild their lives amid miles of rubble. Except for a few streets on the outskirts, there were no traces of the proud, beautiful, cosmopolitan capital of Poland. We walked on streets where the Jewish ghetto was. Not one wall remained. Half a million Jews had lived and perished there.

We were told that only a few Jews were still in the city; a much larger number now made their homes in Lodz, an industrial city which the war had left untouched (because the Germans needed the output of its factories). The Jews we encountered suggested we return to the railway station and go on to Lodz. We took their advice, even though getting on a train was no simple matter in 1945. With help from the resettlement office we managed to do it.

Arriving in Lodz we were astounded to see the city pulsating with life. Right away we met and talked with Jews. They directed us to the Jewish Committee where we registered, got our first good meal in years and received a permit for living quarters.

Many of the Jews in Lodz lived in beautifully furnished apartments, which the Germans had deserted in their flight from the city. They were dressed nicely and had reclaimed some of the factories that belonged to them before the war. Some of the Jews were working at their trades, some speculated on the free market. The Jewish Committee had free kitchens where they extended help to those who came daily to the city in search of fellow Jews.

Being late arrivals, my sister and I were given an un-furnished room and we slept on the bare floor for six weeks. The little money we had we spent for food. Most of the time we ate in the communal kitchen. We were shabbily dressed still, and soon we realized that there was no future for us in Lodz. The most outspoken anti-Semites in Poland, the *Andeki*, had renewed their ugly activities against the Jews. During our six weeks in Lodz, we heard of a couple of minor pogroms on the Jews there. The *Andeki* forced their entry on a few of the prominent Jews and shot them. Some Jews changed their names so they sounded more Polish. Even with the annihilation of almost all of the country's three and a half million Jews, Polish anti-Semitism had not declined. Many Poles were still anxious to kill all of the survivors.

Active in Lodz at the time was the *Bricha*, the Israeli underground which smuggled surviving Jews to Israel. My sister and I made contact with the *Bricha* and got our names on the list. Soon we received orders, along with two dozen other Jews, to go to Krakow, one of Poland's most historic cities. From there, the Israeli underground would smuggle us across the Polish-Czechoslovakian border and then on to Italy or the American Zone in Germany.

In Krakow, when we arrived early in October, the Jewish transit office was located in a large hotel. We were given room and board and told we might have to wait a few days. The last couple of transports had been discovered, we were told. The *Bricha* would have to establish new contacts with the border patrols and alternate routes of passage before it could smuggle us across the border.

Dalya and I were in Krakow for two weeks that were largely uneventful, except for one experience that stands out in my memory. I had persuaded a young man to accompany me to the market on the other side of the city. As we strolled among the peasants, a gypsy fortuneteller called us over. The young man did not believe in fortunetelling, but I was curious, so he waited while the gypsy read my palm. On our way back to the hotel, he noticed that his pockets had been cut and his 2,000 zlotys—all the money he owned—stolen. We felt like such fools—after all we had been through! Because of the absurdity of it, we could not stop laughing all the way back to the hotel.

When the office of the *Bricha* summoned me, I was asked to take charge of a group of 10 people who were to be smuggled out of Poland. Thinking that a man would be better than I for the job, I began to object. The *Bricha* members ignored my protests, considering my underground experiences valuable. I was handed the address of a hotel in Katowice, where the group would spend the night and await further instructions. A bus would pick us up the following morning.

In Katowice, a young man waited to brief us in the lobby of the hotel. We were to go to a railway station, he said, and pretend to be Greeks who were displaced during the war. The young man gave us a letter from the displaced persons' bureau to the commandant at the train station, instructing him to give us passage to Czechoslovakia on our way to Greece. If the police had any suspicion of us—if they asked us any questions—we were to pretend we did not understand Polish. We were to answer in Hebrew, saying whatever came to mind. The Poles knew that the Jews spoke Yiddish but Hebrew was foreign to them, and they might mistake it for Greek.

The railway station was so crowded there was hardly room for our knapsacks. People of all nationalities were spread out on the floor, and among them were many we recognized as Jews. One Jew told us that he, too, was pretending to be Greek and that others were trying to pass as Italians and Yugoslavs. All of them had been in the station for several days but expected to be on a train for Bratislava the next morning.

During the evening, Dalya left the group to look for a toilet. Pretending to be Greek, she couldn't very well ask for directions in Polish so she continued to wander about. She was finally stopped by a policeman. Because of her snooping, he suspected her of being a spy and took her to jail. They kept her there for several hours until she convinced them that finding a toilet was her only mission.

When we gathered the next morning on the train we were crushed together so tightly we could barely move. The heat was suffocating but we were happy to cross the Polish border without incident. As soon as we arrived in Bratislava, we registered in the Joint Distribution Office and were given a bare room in which to sleep.

Bratislava impressed none of us, and we were pleased with our instructions to move on to Prague. It was there, in that beautiful city with its magnificent bridges, that I came face to face with Western civilization. The people were refined and dressed tastefully; at first they seemed almost smug. We could communicate with them to a degree, because the Czech language is closely related to Russian and Polish.

The Czechs were highly cultivated and very courteous to us. The little trouble we did have was due to their mistaking us for Germans when they heard us speaking Yiddish. Their hatred for the Germans was intense, and a couple of times they pushed Jews off moving tramways, thinking they were Germans. Sharing their feelings, we didn't mind taking their punishment. Soon, however, we learned to be very careful not to speak Yiddish in public.

Through the Joint Distribution Office in Prague we had a place to stay, but the problem of food was most disturbing. Food was rationed in Czechoslovakia; without food coupons we could buy nothing and we were constantly hungry. Prague had many beautiful restaurants, in which orchestras and waiters in uniforms with bow ties provided the finishing touches for a sophisticated atmosphere. In our shabby dress, we would go to these restaurants for food. Politely, restaurant employees would explain that they could not serve us without ration coupons. However, we were never turned away without each of us receiving a spoonful of mashed potatoes and gravy.

In the hotel where I stayed, I saw a Negro for the first time in my life. I remember that I was scared at first to look at him. I had learned in school about people of different races and color, but actually seeing a Negro was a strange experience for me. I began to understand that my wanderings were enriching my knowledge. Prague offered me other first experiences: the circus and the zoo. The Prague circus was fantastic and, at the time, was reputed to be the biggest in the world.

Our Prague visit was brief. In two weeks we were on our way to Karlsbad, from where we were to be smuggled across the Czech-German border. By now, our group had become as close to one another as a family, sharing both the good and the bad traveling experiences.

When I beheld Karlsbad, I was struck by its beauty. A small resort town nestled in the mountains, it made such a dazzling impression on me that I was speechless. I marveled at the labrynthian, intricate structure of its streets. At night, when the city was lit up, it looked like a fairy place. No wonder the European royalty had been vacationing there for centuries, enjoying its natural hot spring baths.

Because the Czech-German border was heavily guarded, we were unable to get beyond Karlsbad for several weeks. All kinds of people were trying to stream into the American Zone in Germany. We stayed in what had been a magnificent villa at the very top of the mountain. Fittingly, this transition place for Jews once belonged to a Nazi. But by now—November, 1945—the villa was in shabby condition.

We slept on silk brocaded mattresses infested with bugs. Many of the velvet drapes had been torn down so dresses could be made out of the material.

On the evening of December 4, 1945, when the ten of us tried to speed across the border in a truck, we were forced back by gunfire from the guards. Twice more we tried to cross and failed. When a Czech patrol stopped us for the third time, we confided that we were Jews trying to make it to the American Zone and then to Israel, that we were desperate to leave the European cemetery of six million Jews.

Sympathetic, the patrolmen suggested that we cross the border on foot, through fields two kilometers from the highway. They told us that they would pretend not to notice, and that after a 10-kilometer walk we would arrive in Tirschenreuth, Germany, a small town in the American Zone.

Doing as we were advised, we moved stealthily across plowed fields difficult to walk on. I had lost a shoe jumping over a rivulet and was unable to find it in the darkness. (It seems that shoes are my life's problem.) Once again, the half-frozen ridges of the fields cut into my shoeless foot. I held back the tears and forced myself to keep up with the rest of the group.

We reached Tirschenreuth early in the morning of December 5, 1945. For the first time since the war broke out, we felt like free people. Our fear was replaced by renewed hope for a better future.

When we asked a passerby if any Jews lived in the city, he replied that the only hotel in town had been taken over by the Jews, and he directed us there.

14

The Jewish community of Tirschenreuth numbered about 60 people, all living in a hotel whose lobby served as an office of UNRRA (United Nations Rehabilitation and Relief Agency). Each week the Jewish Committee distributed food packages from UNRRA that were supposed to sustain them for seven days: a loaf of bread, a little cereal, a can of sardines, powdered milk, egg and pea powder, a bit of sugar and, at times, canned meat. You couldn't starve on that ration, nor was it enough to fully satisfy you.

The president of the Jewish Committee, a German Jew, told us that to be registered with UNRRA we would have to say that we were liberated by the American army on German soil. After we did so, we received our displaced person's cards and our food ration.

With the hotel occupied to capacity, we were sent to a huge house adjacent to a convent. Large as it was, it took only a few days for the place to fill up with other refugees. From time to time we went to the convent to ask for an onion or a fresh vegetable, which we could not get from UNRRA. The nuns never refused our requests, but we didn't take advantage of them because they didn't have much themselves.

On Saturday nights, the Jewish Committee held socials,

which even had live music. On one of these nights, two American officers came to visit, one of them a Jew from Chicago who could understand a little Yiddish. When I heard him mention Chicago, I immediately asked him to mail a letter for me to my Chicago relatives. I wanted them to know that Dalya and I had survived the war and were now in Germany.

The young officer was glad to comply and soon afterward brought us a letter with a two-dollar bill from our brother. With the two dollars, I bought myself a pair of shoes—the first pair of my own since 1942. For the next three months the officer visited us on weekends, treating our men to cigarettes and the women with trinkets. Through him we received another letter from our brother suggesting we go to Munich and register with the American consulate for a visa to the States.

Winter and spring passed in idleness but also with the hope that things would soon change for us. Food remained a problem and some of our good friends, with whom we had crossed the borders, could no longer stand the meager and bland diet supplied by UNRRA. Our friend, Mojshe, who had a few dollars, decided to do business on the black market. He bought a cow and sold the meat, turning a nice profit.

Farmers at this time were forbidden by law to sell their cattle without permission from the local government. When Mojshe repeated his illegal business venture, somebody reported him to the police, who immediately came to the hotel to arrest him. Alerted, Mojshe rented a motorcycle and sent a German boy to fetch his wife, Sonya; together, they fled town. After a few days, I received a message from them: a new displaced person's camp was being opened in Furth near Nuremberg; would I bring their belongings and would I pick up a suit that was being made for Mojshe by a German tailor in Tirschenreuth?

I went to the tailor, and he politely asked me to have a

seat. He said the suit was almost finished, that he only had to sew on some buttons. He disappeared and about a half an hour later, two German policemen entered the room and arrested me. With drawn rifles, they hurried me off to the city jail. The charge was "intending to steal." They said they would release me only if I told them the whereabouts of my friend. Of course, I refused. I told them that I was aware only that my friend had given the tailor material to make a suit. Nothing I said would persuade them to let me go; I was forced to await my trial.

The cell, which I shared with a German woman, was dark. The green blankets were rough and foul smelling. Indeed the smell of urine and the filth were so unbearable that I began to throw up blood.

At five in the morning a bell would ring, the door of the cell would open, and the German woman would carry out the night pot. We had only ten minutes to take a cold shower in the filthy hall. On the way back to the cell, I would be given a slice of stale rye bread and a cup of watery soup.

Knowing that Dalya would be worrying, I asked one of the prison guards to let her know where I was. I also asked him to have her get in touch with the president of the Jewish Committee.

Dalya visited me on the third day, bringing a hot meal and assuring me that the Jewish Committee was doing everything possible to obtain my release. The president told her that he needed $50 to bribe the judge. Since we had no money, the president contacted Mojshe, who promised to send $25.

Dalya brought food every day, but she was not allowed inside the prison. We kept in touch through a window in my cell. She kept telling me that the entire Jewish Committee admired me for not betraying Mojshe.

After a week, I was called to the jail office and asked if I wanted a lawyer to represent me. I said that I had done nothing wrong, that I had nothing to fear and that I would defend myself.

The next day, three policemen walked me through the town to the court building. As I was led like a criminal through the streets of this small German town, I thought of the irony of the experience: what a price to pay for surviving the war! If the German police were so firmly set to get out of me the whereabouts of the "Black Marketeer Jew" and so firm against the black market, why didn't they jail their own people? Wasn't it primarily the Germans who bought and sold on the black market?

When I entered the courtroom, I saw Dalya waiting. I was glad to breathe fresh air and sit in a clean room. When I was finally called to the stand, the judge dismissed my case. He did not ask a single question.

Out of jail and united with Dalya, I walked through the lobby of the hotel, where people lined up to shake my hand. I had become a kind of celebrity. That week I was elected to attend the world conference of *Ichud*, a Zionist organization. The conference took place in the huge displaced persons camp in Feldafing, not far from Munich. I took the opportunity to register with the American consulate. Back in Tirschenreuth, I found a letter from Mojshe and Sonya asking my sister and me to settle down with them at Furth. Since we missed them terribly, we agreed to go.

In Furth, at the time of our arrival, the DP camp was in the early stages of formation and Dalya and I received a nicely furnished house to live in. Later, when large numbers of Jewish survivors came streaming in, we had to share our home with a family of five.

But we were happy to be with our friends again. In the evenings, we attended social functions and meetings and listened to speakers from Israel propagate the idea that we all should move there. They were quite successful. Many young people were enlisted and sent to kibbutzim in Germany to prepare for Israeli life.

We had our own dance hall and could take a train to Nuremberg if we wanted to see a movie. Nonetheless, the camp brings back bad memories.

Once while walking with friends in Furth proper, we passed a few frauleins accompanied by American soldiers. The women laughed loudly at us and incited the American soldiers against us. They picked up stones and threw them in our direction, calling "Jude! Jude!"

The encounter crushed our morale and left us completely shaken. It was hard to believe that the Germans, having been soundly defeated, still dared to poison the American soldiers with their hatred of the Jews. Once again, my hopes for a better life and my respect for the human race began to dwindle; had the whole world gone crazy? My mind was so conditioned to fear and distrust that I failed to understand that the soldiers were merely showing off for their German *lieblings*.

We received another shattering blow a short time later. When a German was killed on a train between Furth and Nuremberg, the Jews from our DP camp were blamed for his death. The killer was never apprehended and it is possible that one of our men could not restrain himself from revenge, but after that whenever we boarded the train we were mocked, heckled and sneered at by the Germans.

In my two years in Germany (1945-1947), I remember only one humane gesture from the people. A few German gentlemen, nicely dressed and carrying briefcases, watched me struggling for support on a crowded train and started a conversation with me. Learning I was Jewish, they asked how I survived the war. I explained that I had joined the partisan movement after our ghetto was liquidated. One of the men stood up, bowed deeply and asked to shake my hand.

We were to live in three more locations before leaving for the States: a run-down barracks in a DP camp in Frankfurt, after our camp in Furth was shut down; a kibbutz near the town of Regensburg, where life was communal and we had plenty to eat; a DP camp called *Nei Freiman* where we shared rations and a crowded house with a second cousin of my dear mother, and our cousin's son.

Nei Freiman had its advantages. We used to walk a couple of kilometers to Munich to take in a German movie or to attend the Jewish theater. I enrolled in a commercial school where I learned to type and I took private lessons in English from a young German instructor.

By this time, our passage to America was virtually assured. At the U.S. consulate in Munich I was told that I had received the affidavits from our relatives in Chicago and that Dalya and I would now have to wait for our numbers to come up on the Polish immigration quota.

Meanwhile I applied for a typing job at the UNRRA office and got it. Although I was paid no money for my work, I received additional ration packages and cigarettes. Our situation improved considerably. I did not smoke, so I sold my cigarettes for 200 marks. With the money I bought a few yards of silk and had a seamstress make up a couple of dresses.

Having shed our threadbare clothes, Dalya and I actually looked quite attractive. Being a natural blonde with blue eyes, I looked like a Gentile, a *shiksa*. Because non-Jews were not allowed to enter our camp, I had problems with the guards at the gate. I had to carry my DP identification every time I left.

When a few young men became interested in Dalya and me, we asked our relatives in the States whether we should marry before leaving Europe. In responding, they indicated they did not want to be burdened with additional family responsibilities. They suggested we look around for American men to marry—an unlikely prospect. While

American soldiers fraternized with, courted and even married German girls, the American Jewish soldiers in Germany, as far as I knew, did not try to make acquaintances with the Jewish refugees. Excepting the officer in Tirschenreuth, I had never seen an American Jewish soldier in any of our DP camps.

In March, 1947, Dalya and I were called to the American consulate for a literacy test. Smallpox vaccinations followed, along with chest x-rays and a spraying with delousing powder.

Back at the camp, people were telling us how lucky we were, and their faces revealed an envy that I could not quite understand. Yet, I could not understand my own feelings, so mixed were they with hope and fear. Naturally I was happy to part with the uncertain and idle life of the camps, but I was apprehensive about moving to America—a new and unfamiliar country, with new people, new customs, a new language and acceptance by relatives I didn't really know.

On April 11, 1947, after a two-week wait at the port of Bremen, we boarded the *Marine Perch*. During the war it had been used to transport grain and cattle. In spite of the crude accommodations, it was an exhilarating experience to be at sea for the first time in my life.

The sexes were segregated; even families were separated—the men below decks, the women above. We had 30 to 40 women in one cabin, sleeping on triple-decker bunks.

We left port late in the afternoon and enjoyed a nice evening meal a few hours later. It was the one and only dinner Dalya and I were to eat on the ship. We became seasick the very first night: we could not lift our heads; we were nauseous and everything was spinning about us. There were no stewards to attend to our needs.

The next morning, when an orderly came to tidy up the cabin, I asked for water, which I finally received after several hours. When I got up to search for the washroom, I walked like a drunkard and had to hold on to the railings. Within a day or two, almost everybody on the ship was seasick and the dining room remained empty for the rest of the voyage.

During our 11 days at sea we had only one storm, but it was a bad one. Packages, chairs—everything loose—flew about. The storm raged for an entire evening and Dalya and I truly believed we would not survive it.

On April 23, we heard joyous shouts from the open deck: "Land! We see land!"

As soon as we entered New York harbor, our seasickness ceased, but we felt extremely weak. Late in the evening, we were greeted by representatives of *Hias*, the American Jewish charity group, and allowed off the ship.

As we were driven to the *Hias* house, the city of New York made a dazzling impression on me. Neon signs, moving lights and tall buildings that seemed to touch the night sky left me somewhat bewildered. Open-mouthed and speechless, I kept turning my head from left to right, upward and backward, trying to take in as much of the city as I could on this short trip.

We were given a room for the night and a good breakfast the next morning. The *Hias* had contacted our relatives, who telegraphed money. That very day, we boarded a train and were on our way to Chicago.

Epilogue

Thirty years after the holocaust—no matter how much I have grown to love my adopted homeland, the United States of America—I cannot forget those flames that consumed my faith in humanity. I cannot forget the past, the loved ones whom I have lost forever. Like a plant, a person uprooted this way cannot grow. The life that any refugee tries to build is without foundation.

But I firmly believe there is a purpose in life for the survivors of the holocaust. This purpose is to act as messengers of the massacred six million Jews, to make known to every living human being the terrible truth about the most heinous blood orgy in history. We must remind the free world again and again that race prejudice shrivels the soul. We, the survivors, must never tire of keeping our memories alive.

Three decades have passed since the holocaust, but the world has not changed appreciably. Examples of genocide abound: Biafra, My Lai, the Arab-Israeli conflict. Even my own beloved country, the United States, seems to have developed a taste for domination.

The mother of one soldier involved in the My Lai incident said, "I gave them (the army) a good boy, and they made him a murderer." And one soldier, when asked why he didn't try to stop a buddy from throwing a grenade into a cluster of women and children, replied: "All you had to do was take one look at his face. I think if I had even said a word to him, he would have turned and killed me and not thought a damned thing about it."

Perhaps we should look in the faces of one another to discover why man murders man.

Maybe there is hope in the liberated woman. Maybe she will bring up her children to be free from hate, from war, from competition.

Maybe there is hope in the new generation, educated in a system free from competitiveness and prejudice. Maybe humans will one day find a way to live in relative peace. Only through love, freedom and tolerance can humanity survive.

As for me, there is no forgetting the past that has deprived me of happiness. At every increase of my fortune, at every juncture in my life, my memories turn back to the small world I once knew. And on sleepless nights, *Mein Shtetl Belz*, the song my family sang on warm summer evenings, whispers through my thoughts:

Tell me, old man, tell me swiftly,
Because I want to know everything right now.
Where is the little house that once sparkled?
Does the tree I planted still bloom?

The house is overgrown with thorns and moss,
The old roof is buckled,
The windows are paneless,
The stoop is sunken,
The walls are bent.
You won't recognize it anymore.

Belz, my little town, Belz,
My home, where my youthful years I spent,

Epilogue

Belz, my little town, Belz,
In the poor little house,
With all the children I laughed.
Every Sabbath I ran with the prayer book,
To read it under the green tree by the
streamlet.
Belz, my deal little town, Belz,
The home that nourished me
And the many beautiful dreams I dreamed.